Folklore and Traditional Music
in the Former Soviet Union and Eastern Europe

Proceedings of a One-Day Conference, May 16, 1994
sponsored by
the Department of Ethnomusicology and
the Center for European and Russian Studies,
under the auspices of
the International Studies and Overseas Programs, UCLA

Edited by James Porter

Assistant Editors:
David Borgo
Paulette Gershen
Ellen Sinatra

Department of Ethnomusicology, UCLA

1997

Cover Design: Daniel Shiplacoff

ISBN : 0-88287-054-8

Folkore and Traditional Music
in the Former
Soviet Union and Eastern Europe

CONTENTS

vi

Conference Participants

RONELLE ALEXANDER is Professor of Slavic Languages and Literatures at the University of California, Berkeley. Her field is South Slavic language, literature, Slavic linguistics, and Slavic and East European folklore. Among her research interests are Balkan linguistics, orality and literacy, and Slavic accentology. She has published most recently on the poetics of Vuk Karadzic's Kosovo songs (1991) and on the evolution of South Slavic prosodic systems (1993).

MAGDA ZELINSKA FERL is former Professor with the Union Institute, Los Angeles and served as General Secretary for the Slovak World Congress. Her UCLA dissertation deals with the concept of ethnicity and discusses the traditional arts as a means of expressing ethnicity. She has presented numerous academic papers on Slavic traditional arts and music and has published several articles on Slavic culture, notably Czech and Slovak, including "Folklore and Government Sponsored Festivals." She currently is a freelance educator in Los Angeles and teaches extension classes at UCLA.

IRINA GUTKIN holds degrees from Moscow State University, Columbia University, and UC Berkeley. She is Assistant Professor in the Department of Slavic Languages and Literatures at UCLA, where she teaches courses on Russian literature. Her general research interests lie in the intersection of literature, history and ideology in the Russian cultural context. She is currently completing a book on the cultural roots of Socialist Realism. In folklore she has worked on the potential influence of the long *bylina* (folk epic) verse line on the expansion of the funeral lament line in the repertoire of women lamenters who also became singers of the *bylina*.

BARBARA KIRSHENBLATT-GIMBLETT is Professor of Performance Studies in the Tisch School of the Arts and Professor of Hebrew and Judaic Studies at New York University. She is a Past President of the American Folklore Society and has been a J. Paul Getty Scholar at the Getty Center for the History of Art and the Humanities. Her publications include *Image Before My Eyes: A Photographic History of Jewish Life in Poland, 1864–1939* (with Lucjan Dobroszycki), which formed the basis for a major museum exhibition and feature documentary film. Her most recent book, *Destination Culture: Tourism, Museums, and Heritage*, will appear in 1997 (University of California Press).

ALMA KUNANBAEVA was born in Almaty, Kazakhstan, and is Associate Professor in the Department of Traditional Cultures, St. Petersburg Pedagogical University. She has specialized in field studies of Kazakh music and epic song, and has published numerous articles and encyclopedia entries on this material. She has been invited to hold seminars outside Russia: at the Freie Universität, Berlin; the Georg-August Universität, Göttingen; and in the United States at Yale, Columbia, Ohio State University, and the Universities of Maryland, Pennsylvania, Washington, and Wisconsin. In 1994-97 she is teaching at the University of Wisconsin, Madison.

ANKICA PETROVIC was educated at the University of Sarajevo and studied for her doctoráte in ethnomusicology in Belfast, Northern Ireland with the noted scholar John Blacking. She has been a Fellow at the National Humanities Center, Chapel Hill (1993–94), has taught at Duke University and UC Berkeley, and is Visiting Professor at UCLA in 1996–97. Her main research interests are in theory and method in ethnomusicology, ethnicity in music, and music and gender. She has also made a special study of religious chant (Catholic, Orthodox, Muslim, and Sephardic) and has published widely on traditional and contemporary musical practices in the Balkans and Near East.

TIMOTHY RICE is Professor of Ethnomusicology at UCLA. A specialist in the traditional music of Bulgaria and the former Yugoslavia, he has done extensive fieldwork in both areas since 1969. He has been Editor of the journal *Ethnomusicology* and is currently co-editing the *Europe* volume of the *Garland Encyclopedia of World Music*. He has published articles in the major ethnomusicology journals, and his book *May It Fill Your Soul: Experiencing Bulgarian Music* was recently published by the University of Chicago Press.

CAROL SILVERMAN is Associate Professor of Anthropology and Folklore and served as Director of the Russian and East European Studies Center at the University of Oregon. Her research focuses on the politics of culture, especially the interplay between official and countercultural spheres in music and ritual. She has done fieldwork with Muslim minorities for over twenty years in Bulgaria and Macedonia, and also with Balkan-Americans. She is a specialist in Rom (Gypsy) folklore, has published numerous articles on this topic, and works in the area of human rights.

MARK SLOBIN is Professor of Music at Wesleyan University and a former president of both the Society for Ethnomusicology and the Society for Asian Music. He is the author of numerous books on world musics including *Subcultural Sounds: Micromusics of the West* (Wesleyan University Press, 1993), and he recently edited the volume *Retuning Culture: Musical Changes in Central and Eastern Europe* (Duke University Press, 1996).

IZALY ZEMTSOVSKY is former Department Head in Folklore, Russian Institute for the History of the Arts, St. Petersburg. In the same city, he remains affiliated with the Russian Pedagogical University and Petersburg Jewish University and is Chair of the Folklore Department in the Union of Russian Composers. Among his many accomplishments, he has been named an Honored Person of the Arts of Russia (1991) and has published some fifteen books on Russian and Slavic folk music, and more than 400 articles in Russian, Bulgarian, German, Romanian, and English-language scholarly journals. He has given lectures in a number of countries, including Austria, Finland, the Georgian Republic, Germany, the former Yugoslavia, and the United States. In 1997-98, he will be Visiting Professor at University of California Berkeley .

Preface and Acknowledgements

The idea for this conference stemmed from the happy confluence of a number of circumstances, in particular the presence at UCLA of Professor Izaly Zemtsovky during the Spring Quarter, 1994. As Chair of the Department I had invited Dr. Zemtsovsky to teach two graduate courses for us that quarter. Similarly, I knew that Dr. Petrović happened to be in the United States as a Visiting Scholar at the National Humanities Center, Chapel Hill, having recently left war-torn Bosnia. The convenient visits of Professors Kirshenblatt-Gimblett and Mark Slobin to Los Angeles at that time added to the notion that a one-day conference might be possible. Professors Carol Silverman and Ronelle Alexander also readily agreed to attend from their West Coast locations in Eugene and Berkeley respectively. Finally, we had some enthusiastic support from colleagues in both the Department of Slavic Languages and our own School of the Arts. I am grateful to Professors Irina Gutkin, Michael Heim, Timothy Rice, and Dr. Magda Zelinska-Ferl for their participation.

The conference theme of the Status of the Traditional Arts and Music in the Former Soviet Union and Eastern Europe seemed timely as well as urgent. We were extremely fortunate to have with us at this conference scholars of such distinction in their respective fields. In publishing these proceedings we are offering, perhaps, some illumination—through expert and perceptive analysis—of the ways in which the traditional arts and folk culture interact with politics, especially radical political organization such as occurred in those regions following two World Wars.

The conference itself was readily funded by the School of the Arts through Dean Robert Blocker, and we thank him for his generosity. I also owe a debt of thanks to Dr. Ivan Berend, director of the Center for European and Russian Studies, UCLA for his unstinting interest and support.

James Porter

Conference Program

9.00 A.M.   **Welcoming Remarks**
Robert L. Blocker, Dean of the School of the Arts, UCLA

9:05 A.M.   **Introduction to the Conference**
James Porter, Chair, Department of Ethnomusicology,
UCLA

9.10 A.M.   **Session I: Russia and the Fomer Soviet Union**
Moderator: Michael Heim, Department of Slavic Languages & Literatures, UCLA

9.15 A.M.   **Key Paper: Socialism and Folklore**
Izaly Zemtsovsky, Russian Institute for History of the
Arts, St. Petersburg, Russia
Alma Kunanbaeva, St. Petersburg Pedagogical University

10.00 A.M.   Response:
Barbara Kirshenblatt-Gimblett, Department of Performance Studies, New York University

10.20 A.M.   Response
Mark Slobin, Department of Music, Wesleyan University

10.40 A.M.   Response:
Irina Gutkin, Department of Slavic Languages & Literatures, UCLA

11.00 AM   **Open Discussion**

Lunch

2.00 P.M.	**Session II: East and East-Central Europe** Moderator: James Porter, Department of Ethnomusicology, UCLA
2.05 P.M.	**Key Paper: The Status of Traditional Music in Eastern Europe** Ankica Petrović, National Humanities Center, Chapel Hill
2.50 P.M.	Response: Carol Silverman, Department of Anthropology, University of Oregon
3.10 P.M.	Response: Timothy Rice, Department of Ethnomusicology, UCLA
3.30 P.M.	Response: Magda Zelinska-Ferl, Union Institute, Los Angeles
3.50 P.M.	**Open discussion**
4.40 P.M.	Concluding Remarks: Ronelle Alexander, Department of Slavic Languages & Literatures, UC Berkeley

Reception: Schoenberg Hall patio

Part One: The Former Soviet Union

IZALY ZEMTSOVSKY
ALMA KUNANBAEVA

Communism and Folklore

Talk not of seventy years as age; in seven
I have seen more changes, down from monarchs
To the humblest individual under heaven,
Than might suffice a moderate century through.
I knew that nought was lasting, but now even
Change grows too changeable, without being new...

(Byron, *Don Juan*, canto 11, stanza 81)

Don't spare us [Russians]: we forget our
situation too quickly, we too easily become
accustomed to amusing ourselves within
the walls of our prison...

(Alexander Hertzen, *On the Development of
Revolutionary Ideas in Russia*, 1850)

Let us start with an explanation of the title because of its present-day double meaning. In fact, for Westerners "the fall of communism" means the fall of Soviet socialism, i.e., the collapse of the USSR as the stronghold of the phenomenon usually known in Russia as "socialism" (and "developed" or "mature socialism") but never as "communism." We knew only the form "socialism," which was represented by the Soviet regime itself. For us, "communism" was more a radiant future than a matter of our everyday life. There were very few people who truly understood the essence of our self-styled official expression, the "Communist Party of the Soviet Union," as something that treated the reality of "communism à la Soviet." For Russian readers, therefore, our title "Communism and Folklore" means something very futurological and idealistic, such as "Folklore in the Conjectural Radiant Future," whereas for Western readers it means something very concrete that has already been accomplished, such as "Folklore in the Dark Soviet Past" or, more precisely, folklore during the whole Soviet era.

This period, paradoxically, was anticipated by Byron's brilliant lines from *Don Juan* as though they were purposely written about the 70 years' existence of the Soviet Union and the seven years of post-Soviet *perestroika* . To be a chronicler of that epoch is difficult and burdensome. Alexander Hertzen helps us overcome such a mood with the bitter phrase we have quoted as a second epigraph.

Briefly we can state that there were two evils in the USSR: 1) a sharp divergence between theory and practice, i.e., too much unrestrained verbal demagogy and monstrous repression in actual fact; and 2) the coincidence of theory and practice, when theory was made a tool of authority and was forcibly put into effect, i.e., when we were terrified in word and deed.

Thus, throughout the entire life span of the Soviet regime there were striking contradictions between the socialism of official propaganda and the version of socialism that was actually put into practice. It was as though there existed two separate ideologies. While one ideology was a guide for action, the other served as a curtain behind which the regime shielded its true intentions. Passing off one as the other for decades, the regime never admitted the existence of these two theories—one that was practiced and the other that provided a beautiful but treacherous smokescreen to hide a frightening reality. There is an anecdote that paraphrases a line from Vladimir Mayakovsky's poem "Lenin," which everyone knew in the Russia of one's schooldays. The line reads: "We say 'Lenin' and imply the '[Communist] Party.' We say 'Party' and imply 'Lenin.' And the entire seventy years of the Soviet regime are like this—we say one thing but imply another." Westerners know this from *The Russians* by Hedrick Smith, who quotes a typical Soviet saying: "When I make a speech, it sounds just right. But what I say and what I am thinking when I am saying it are two different things" (1976:364).

Nowhere are the tragic contradictions between Soviet socialist theory and life more evident than in the sphere of folklore. The true status of folklore under the Soviet regime was far removed from the official position maintained in the cultural arena. Officially and forcefully, folklore was proclaimed to hold an exalted status. This demagogic ideology referred to folklore as "the people's creative work" (this Soviet formula was extremely popular during the last 60 years), claiming that it expressed the free creative will of the diligent builders of socialism. Folklore could therefore be viewed as the foundation of socialist culture as a whole; it was the source of all that was best, and only the best, in culture. Consequently, folklore should be the best in and of itself; it should be Soviet enough. Furthermore, the members of the intelligentsia (who were not a part of "the people" but were an opposing stratum of society) were told to learn from folklore and to extrapolate from it.

Thus, in words and on paper, folklore was respected and supported; but in fact, the Soviet government actively supported its own version of folklore. However, this particular version had little to do with the people's free creativity and everything to do with the regime's aim of total control of all cultural activities. We remember the story of a Lithuanian colleague from the 1950s and 1960s. She said that the local branch of the KGB sent for their ethnomusicologists and gave them a piece of good advice, saying: "We will permit you to study your folklore; be happy, but please, do not propagandize the traditional culture, do not invite students and the young generation at all into your fieldwork, do not organize special ethnographic concerts, and do not establish new folklore ensembles in the cities! Be quiet and calm; for the time being we will tolerate you!"

At the First Congress of Soviet Writers in 1934, Maxim Gorky, the leading Soviet writer of that time, first expressed the notion that folklore was the creative work of not just any people, but of the "laboring masses." The notion was so ideologically oriented that it became fraught with many dangerous but practical consequences and results. Such results were not long in coming. Gorky's concept was very close to a well-known phrase of Lenin's, who defined folklore as expressing the interests, thoughts and aspirations of the working people. In principle it was clear that only manual labor was regarded as work. According to such a doctrine, religious thought was alien to folklore: true folklore supposedly stood in opposition to Christianity and Islam (not to mention Judaism!) and mocked both the priest and the mullah (not to mention the rabbi!). Certainly, folklore had to disdain the landowner, and the tsar as well. Stylistically, folklore under socialism necessarily belonged to the category of realism, meaning that its form had to be easily accessible to the working masses. Furthermore, the restrictions imposed by the official definition resulted in the so-called "declassed elements" (including the entire population of the GULAG) having no "folklore" at all. Anything created by them went conspicuously unnoticed. Folklore under socialism was to be truly "socialist," that is, in the eyes of the regime "pure," but in reality, sterile.

Socialism boasted of the "free creativity of the people," while in truth the creativity it supported and propagandized came from individuals who were controlled and organized to the highest degree. Officially sanctioned "amateur circles" (*samodeyatel'nost'*) and extravagant folklore festivals promoted only what was carefully selected and approved by Soviet officials. The strictest censorship was imposed on everything that was published and performed, including every sound that was played.

The efforts to control folklore, however, went beyond simply limiting what could be presented. The "amateur artistic activity" that the regime so prominently supported consisted, for the most part, of an imagined folklore, one fabricated by socialism for its own purposes. There actually existed a system of made-to-order folklore, under which obedient scholars and frightened performers produced folklore on command, sometimes under the threat of immediate physical violence. Imagine being ordered at gunpoint to create a folksong! It was this fabricated folklore (new songs (*noviny*) about our new life, as opposed to old songs (*byliny* or *stariny*) about the past) that began to take the place of genuine folk art. A Western reader can learn today about the "new" Russian folklore from Frank Miller's book, which has the wonderful title *Folklore for Stalin: Russian Folklore and Pseudofolklore of the Stalin Era.*

Folklore in the USSR was called upon to help in the building of a new culture, "national in form and socialist in content" (this formulation of Stalin's was applied to folklore as well as to other areas of Soviet life). Whatever and whoever did not suit this model was to be reoriented or eliminated. Academics in the field of folklore had to bring their writings into line with the regime's aims or suffer moral and/or even physical abuse. Entire peoples and genres were persecuted and, in some cases, destroyed through the government's efforts to purify folklore. The epic created in the epoch of feudalism, shamanism, religious art, oral professionalism connected with traditional court and palace life, traditional rites connected with the religious calendar, and even jokes, were all victims in this unequal struggle.

In essence, the history of socialism and folklore is the history of socialism's attempts to destroy folklore under the pretext of its preservation. Fortunately, socialism did not fully succeed in realizing any of its plans fully, including the annihilation of genuine folklore. Totalitarianism brought about a deformation of culture and cultural life. Restricted by numerous regulations adopted by the State authorities and the Party bodies, culture was not allowed to develop naturally. These restrictions and persecutions were taboos which led, quite logically, to the rise of a creative underground at all levels, in terms of meaning and form in the oral and written arts, including folklore and the music of oral tradition.

Despite the regime's efforts to destroy it, unofficial folklore survived and bore fruit in the USSR. Fortunately, many aspects of traditional culture had survived already for centuries and could not be extinguished even by the most violent means. Beyond this was the unofficial folklore that arose as a direct response to modern life and reality. Some of the more productive forms during the Soviet period were the rhymed, sung couplets or quatrains (*chastushkas*), jokes and anecdotes, pithy expressions, reworking of familiar songs and poems, urban songs, student lore, and the folklore of the GULAG.

The first "Folklore of the GULAG" conference took place in St. Petersburg, as recently as November 1992. The conference proceedings, compiled by Vladimir Bakhtin and Boris Putilov and edited by Vladimir Lurie, were published in *Folklore and Cultural Environment of the GULAG* (1994). The organizers of the conference attempted, for the first time in Russia, to include under the category of "folklore" the entire body of expressive culture which arose and was in use among prisoners in prison camps, in Nazi camps, labor camps, and prisons; in ghettoes; among citizens under investigation, deported family members, the residents of special children's homes, and children's penal colonies—among all those who in various eras and circumstances were victims of the totalitarian communist regime.

It is worth knowing that five groups of genres have been included: verbal culture in all its variety (legends, lore, stories, anecdotes, jokes, songs, *chastushkas,* proverbs, catch-phrases, nicknames, expressions for situations specific to the GULAG), all terminology and slang referring to objects, actions, deeds, behavior, relationships, calls and signals, obscenities, and the like; musical and musical/verbal material, self-made musical instruments; kinesthetic material (the language of gesture, mimicry, forms of "etiquette"); theatrical or dramatic culture, as well as various forms of impersonation and mimicry; representational culture (e.g., tattoos and symbols, in addition to drawings and paintings). As long as it is authentic, even the most insignificant material is of historical and cultural value today. We refer to the vibrant spectrum of material that comprised the oral culture of the GULAG and provided its prisoners with a means of survival, resistance, and expression of thoughts and feelings.

Such a richness today seems self-evident, but we must remember that these statements were made in the seventh year of *perestroika*! It was terribly difficult to break through the totalitarian concepts that had become our flesh and blood during those long years.

The present situation in the fields of folklore and folkloristics, as well as in ethnomusicology, may be said to have resulted from State policy and the ideology practiced in those fields until the advent of *perestroika*. In its turn, State policy may be said to have resulted from three basic fears inherent to a totalitarian regime, fears that we will formulate as follows: fear of oral tradition, since it is barely noticeable, dramatically out of control, and practically not submissive to any authority or censor; fear of personality, of anyone being one's own person, since such persons are unpredictable and stand out from any solid, uniform, authorized, or dependable collective body, whereas official folklore was established under the Soviets as a stable standard to be imitated and followed unwaveringly; fear of the national uniqueness of other peoples, whose national folklore is quite different from the standard, sterilized, official folklore of their "elder brother," the Russian people. (Incidentally, in this context Lenin's formula for communism as "Soviet power plus electrification of the entire country" may very well be read as "Soviet power plus Russification of the entire country.")

It goes without saying that living folklore was continuously suppressed in this atmosphere of terror. Instead, the State was busy implanting something reliable and politically trustworthy, namely a thing called "people's creative art of written tradition." We even had a special series of books entitled *Sovremennoye Russkoye Narodnoye Pis'mennoye Tvorchestvo* (Modern Russian Folk Literary Creativity). This was effected by issuing instructions and manuals, lists of recommended repertoire (where "recommended" means "in the form of an order"), authorized collections of folksongs, and, above all, by entrusting the task of directing all folk choirs and orchestras to specially trained "leaders of folk choirs or orchestras." They had the word "folk" in the title of their occupation, but they had nothing to do with true folklore. Thirty-five pompous Ten-Day Festivals of "national arts" were staged in Moscow from 1936 to 1960, merely for show and propaganda. These music and dance events were performed in conjunction with the well-known "All-Union Exhibition for Achievements of National Economy," a huge exhibition of buildings representing each national republic in the Soviet Union (so-called VDNX). In brief, folklore was generally replaced by fakelore (cf. Richard Dorson's concept that contrasts folklore and fakelore in his 1976 book of the same title). Genuine folklore traditions were studied by a few academics working in the "permitted" fields of folkloristics and ethnomusicology, and were limited mainly to the so-called peasant legacy. The results of their painstaking research were published in doses so small that most people had no access to them.

Soviet folkloristics came to be based on a publication by Lenin's fellow Bolshevik, Vladimir Bonch-Bruyevich. His paper, "Lenin on the People's Oral Art" was published in 1954 and since then was traditionally quoted—as a classic work—by every writer in the field.[1]

There have been many publications devoted to Lenin. In 1983, a special reference book was published by A. Aleksandrov that contained an authorized list of exemplary works to be performed or studied. It was entitled *Lenin in the Folklore of the Soviet Peoples*. One of us (Zemtsovsky 1971) did his duty and published a similar collection to mark the centenary of our leader. He had do this in order to launch a new series of research papers, "Folklore and Folkloristics." (We should point out that the series is very much alive but has long ago shaken off all political and ideological implications.)

The culmination of the ideological era of folklore studies was reached with the 1980 publication of a Ph.D. dissertation by M. Rusin. In this work, "The Problem of Aesthetic Criteria in Modern Folklore," Rusin took pleasure in stating the main achievement of communist policy in the field of folklore: namely, folklore was made manageable and easily controlled, it had been tamed, it had been converted (at last!) from its natural state into a Party form of art, and it had been substituted for so-called professional art. Rusin wrote, "Under mature socialism, folklore is composed in the same forms—and according to the same rules—that are active in professional art. The boundaries of modern folk art cannot be defined by the basic characteristics of traditional folklore."

The Communist Party prided itself on such an "evolution" of folklore. In 1949 the loyal Party folklorist Vladimir Chicherov (1906-1956) wrote these words, "The Party press is at the head of folk art and is, not infrequently, the source of mass works of art created by the people." Chicherov knew such things first-hand because he himself had applied arm-twisting tactics, compelling storytellers and epic singers from the Russian North to compose—to "create," so to speak—new songs about new Soviet leaders and official heroes. Chicherov himself "called the tune" in the field of folk tradition on behalf of the Communist Party. Fortunately, we were able to learn much from the late Russian ethnomusicologist Yevgeny Hippius (1903–1985)—in Russian, Evgenii Vladimirovich Gippius—who was, without a doubt, a living chronicle and personification of the annals of Soviet folkloristics and ethnomusicology. Hippius recounted privately in his Moscow home not long before his death how Chicherov invited well-known folk narrators (including the epic singer Marfa Krjukova [1876–1954] who, even after that, became a member of the Soviet Writers' Union) to Moscow, locked them alone in a separate room, then threatened everyone with deportation to Siberia, thus reminding them of the Soviet campaign to eliminate the rich farmers (*kulaks*) as a class. If that were not yet enough, he terrified them with a revolver. He did this while demanding that upon his return in six hours, the new song be ready for recording as a free expression of the people's will.

However hidden it may have been from everyone, such extortion of "folklore" had a long official prehistory in Soviet Russia. As far back as 1919, Lenin issued a decree ordering the People's Commissariat for Education to control and to be responsible for all popular amusement and entertainment. In 1925 a songbook for schools was published, offering music by Robert Schumann and Johannes Brahms. It featured communist texts specially written to glorify the young pioneers and the dawn of freedom gained in October 1917, the year of the Great October Revolution, as it began to be called somewhat later. As early as 1918, Lenin officially launched a pompous project for communist propaganda and agitation by means of art and folklore. The well-known Soviet folklorist Yuri Sokolov (1889-1941) wrote in his book *Russian Folklore* (1966:141): "Never, in all the history of Russia, has the oral poetic word served the social aims so broadly and powerfully as in the Soviet period. Soviet folkloristics has helped to reveal the agitational and propagandist significance of folklore." In 1933 a circular was sent out to all those concerned with strict instructions, a kind of user's guide to the organization of public holidays and festivals. This circular also contained a minimal list of five songs to be learned and sung by the working masses: "The International," "The Comintern," "Bravely, Comrades, Walk in Step," "The Guerrilla Song," and "Song about Head-Wind." Even before that, in 1929, a regulated handbook was published for the Komsomol (Young Communist League) members to be trained in mass music. They were officially called *zateinik* (inciter, instigator, organizer of entertainments, i.e., proletarian jester). In 1948, the notorious year of the special Communist Resolution against formalism in music, a "set of new problems" was formulated not by but for "ethnologists" (cultural anthropologists) and folklorists from above "in connection with the current state of affairs at the musical front." The military notion "front" subsequently became very popular among Soviet art critics, musicologists, and folklorists. Step by step the Communist Party went on the offensive against authentic folklore tradition. After World War II "the secret was out," and in 1950 the Agitation and Propaganda Department of the Communist Party of the Soviet Union (*Kommunisticheskaya Partiya Sovetskogo Sojuza*) Central Committee held a special meeting to discuss the modern folksong, including discussion of the means of recording folksongs, and means of adopting, and propagandizing folksongs. Traditional songs and traditional music-making were disdained and suppressed. All over the country, innumerable lists of recommended "folklore" repertoire were published and strenuously distributed, with instructions to all organized folklore groups. This campaign was so important for officials that even much later, in 1979,

Alexey Manayenkov submitted and defended a Ph.D. dissertation, "Party Leadership in Developing the Culture of Rural Districts under Mature Socialism." According to Soviet ideology, the more "leadership," the more "mature" the complaisant "folklore tradition" would become.

In the same post-war period, other folklore scholars and ethnomusicologists (at that time in Russia they were called musical folklorists) wrote about the then-fashionable notion of "folklore evolution," obsequiously stating that the passage from the oral tradition into a written one did not mean eradicating true folklore from people's memories—it was, they said, a higher stage of folklore development (Aksjuk 1962). They declared there was nothing to worry about and that things were going correctly, for according to communist doctrine any development could only be progressive in the USSR. This development, however, was painstakingly guided from above—Folklore should be recommended and used selectively. Yuri Sokolov wrote in the 1930s: "Before us stands the task of a critical review of all of the cultural heritage in oral creativity of the city and the countryside. We must rework and develop that which helps socialist construction and the growth of proletarian culture" (Howell 1992:270).

The 1930s saw the beginning of "innovations" introduced into folklore as a response to the appeal for "revolutionary men of culture" to take an active participation in creating new forms of folklore, in developing a new folklore, and in cultivating it. In fact, this was the beginning of a real struggle—at the State level—for the so-called promotion of folklore arts (or folk art, as we prefer to say in Russia). All-Union assemblies were held for folksingers to encourage them in all possible ways, especially by presenting them with the highest State awards. Thus, the Order of Lenin was bestowed for the performance of songs and epics about Lenin, Stalin, the affluent collective farm (*kolkhoz*), and the State as the "warmly-loved homeland or fatherland." All this was a clear example of a "carrot-and-stick" policy.

In 1937, the first substantial collection of such "innovations" was published with the due authorization of the CPSU Central Committee. As a result, the terrible year 1937, the year of the biggest "purge" and bloodshed in the history of communist Russia, came to be called by the musical press the "Golden Age for the people's creative work" (e.g., in the writing of Georgy Khubov, who used this popular Soviet formula for such a demagogic slogan). At the same time, amateur clubs, societies, agitation brigades, and various collectives of "artistic activity" were set up all over the country. They were expected to prove that a truly professional standard could be attained only "from above," i.e., by copying "classic models" of written musical (composed) and poetic (literary) traditions—from new

European point of view—existing both in Russia and in the West but alien to all living oral traditions. When they were allowed to be performed, folklore pieces were specially adapted so as to be caricatures. All this led to a mental shift in the people's perception of folklore and their perceptive powers and cultural ideals in general. Under the pressure of intimidation, people performed only those pieces that they knew would be approved by the authorities and for which the performers would be handsomely awarded. Consequently, true folklore was deliberately and despicably distorted.

Immediately after World War II, authorized lists of "innovations" began to be published regularly, while theoreticians of the new trend, such as Sergey Aksjuk, wrote about a "perfectly new, unprecedented phenomenon" and a "desire to introduce an organizing factor into the process of people's creative work" (Aksjuk 1950). Now, especially after the statements of Yevgeny Hippius quoted earlier, we know what that factor really was: innovations were really composed at gunpoint or with a threat of imminent exile; i.e., the so-called new folklore was fabricated by the methods of the secret police.

The theory and practice of class struggle and of jingoism were applied to folklore. We would like to quote one paragraph from the outwardly innocent book entitled *Music in the Museum*, edited by the famous Hermitage (the former Winter Palace, a residence of the Russian tsar) Museum in 1934. On page 34 one reads: "In the final account, the struggle between different types of musical instruments always and everywhere existed as a mirror of the general class struggle in the musical field." (At that time these words sounded almost the same as "musical front.") We can state that this did not concern everyday life and that the very idea of folklore had become taboo; it was isolated from all kinds of aesthetic, ideological, social, and class-oriented limitations. Even such a prominent public figure as Anatoly Lunacharsky, the People's Commissar for Education, published an article on the most widely popular of the Russian epic heroes and called it "Ilya Muromets as a Revolutionary" (1919). In order to be a contemporary hero, a real folklore hero had to become a revolutionary.

The same policy was carried out in regard to religion: everything was to be transformed and exposed. New collections of songs were offered to the Russian Orthodox public, such as *Komsomol Christmas* (1923, published by Krasnaya Nov') or *Komsomol Easter Songs* (1923, published by Tulgubkom GKSB). The then-popular monthly, *The Red Magazine for Everyone* (1922) published a selection of *chastushkas* by the proletarian poet (and at that time a folklorist of the new generation) Vasily Knyazev under the heading of *Red Chastushkas about the Red Revolution*. Obviously, folklore and folkloristics became red in the Soviet Union after the Revolution. (We would have liked to see them become red with shame.)

At the beginning of the 1930s, communist folklorists also wrote that traditional folklore had become an alien element which was as outdated as the ancient four-wheeled cart. Folklore ought to be replaced by new songs, which would be as definite an improvement on the old forms as the tractor was on the cart. In truth, Soviet policy underwent changes shortly thereafter. Instructions were issued to collect songs of oral tradition among workers, peasants, and Red Army men, since only these three classes were considered to be representative of the people (the people, of course, as defined by Marxism-Leninism). Later, in 1945, an All-Union competition of patriotic songs and epics was announced. The event led to the publication of new patriotic songs. One of the first collections was edited by the loyal Party folklorist Victor Gusev in Chelyabinsk in 1948.

Meanwhile, State authorities began to suppress all reluctant and unrepentant folklorists and performers, and even "contradictory" folklore works themselves. For example, in 1944 the CPSU Central Committee decided to ban the Tartar epic poem "Idigey" because it glorifies feudalism and the rulers of the community (*khan*). This was immediately followed by a ban on all similar epics composed under "backward," "dark," "obscure" feudalism, because the epic heroes of that period were personalities of whom the Bolsheviks disapproved. Thus the epics of most Turkic-speaking peoples, including not only those situated on the Volga but also throughout Central Asia and most of the Caucasus, were not allowed to be performed, translated, published, or studied. Perhaps the only exceptions were the Russian heroic-patriotic *bylina* and *novina* that became our national pride and a standard part of every school reader.

Many talented performers of epics and shamans' invocations, masters of oral professionalism (i.e., of such high genres of oral tradition as the Uzbek and Tajik *makom* or the Ukrainian epics, *dumy*) were suppressed. We still do not have documentary publications about this horrible practice. Only recently, two articles by the American scholar William Noll on Ukrainian *kobza*-players were published, in the *Folklife Center News* of the Library of Congress, and in the new Ukrainian journal *Rodovid* (whose editor is Lidia Lukhach, Kiev). There are several other reliable publications in this magazine. Allow us to quote a paragraph from Dr. Noll's letter addressed to Dr. Zemtsovsky on March 28, 1994:

> Publications on this topic are both timely and important. I
> am sure you would agree, that too many of our colleagues in

Western Europe and North America have an absurdly positive opinion about the history and role of state financed
music and culture control under the communists. Throughout Eastern Europe, but especially in the lands of the old
USSR, the evidence suggesting a different kind of opinion
is enormous. This evidence is not known abroad. For example, who in the USA knows about [Kliment] Kvitka's
arrest and years in prison in the 1930s? I don't know if the
name Borys Luhovs'kyi is familiar to you, but we included
unpublished materials of his in the enclosed issue of *Rodovid*.
He was an active fieldworker in Chernihiv in the 1920s.
They arrested him the first time in 1926. They arrested him
a second time in 1937. While sitting in prison waiting for his
political trial to begin, he hanged himself. [Gnat] Khotkevych
was shot. [Andrij] Hvylia was shot. Katerina Hrushevs'ka
died in labor camp—and on and on the list goes. There are
so many examples of scholars repressed and/or killed that it
is sometimes overwhelming—this is a difficult topic, emotionally draining. It strains the imagination to believe that
such things were not only possible, but that some of those
who committed these crimes were so highly honored for
them by their colleagues, and that so many of our colleagues
today refuse to believe or try to understand what happened.
(Noll 1994)

To a considerable extent this telltale document might be expanded
to include materials of all other former Soviet republics and national
cultures. For instance, the ethnomusicologist Mikhail Kondrat'yev
(Cheboksary) recently published some information about mass repressions
in the 1930s among Chuvash musicians who were prosecuted as "national-
ists" and "counter-revolutionaries," including Stepan Maksimov, the great-
est folklorist and ethnomusicologist of the Chuvash Republic. The
ethnomusicologist Shakhym Gullyev (Ashgabad), in response to our re-
quest, sent us a preliminary list of repressed and outstanding Turkmen epic
singers (*bakhshi*) and shamans (*porkhan*) shot at the end of the 1930s,
including those from the oldest Merv province: Mukhammetmurat Nepesliev,
Nobat-bakhshi, Khydyr-bakhshi. In order to save himself, Karli-bakhshi
Sultanov crossed over to Afghanistan where he remained to the end of his
life.

In the case of Kazakhstan, we have an excellent dictionary of traditional epic singers and storytellers that enumerates about 35 personalities who died as a result of persecution, starvation, or repression during the 1920s and 1930s (see *Akyn-Zhyraular* by Mardan K. Baidildaev, Almaty 1979, in Kazakh). Among them was such an outstanding singer-poet (*zhyrau*) as Iztileutov Turmagambet (1882–1939), who was well known in particular as the translator of "Shakh-name" into Kazakh.

The elimination of the national intelligentsia began in the 1930s with the epic singers (*zhyrau*) in Kazakhstan. In the past they were influential people in that traditional society as advisers to the *khan* or spiritual leaders of the community. The Soviet regime consciously reduced their status to that of an ordinary all-Union amateur activity. This monstrous transformation had disastrous consequences for the whole traditional culture and its social institutions.

Even some musical instruments were repressed during the 1930s. For example, the fiddle was condemned as a bourgeois instrument in the Ukraine. In many Ukrainian villages, traditional fiddles were destroyed piece by piece: they were broken up into worthless logs. Consequently, an end came to the famous Ukrainian instrumental groups (*troista muzyka*), and Jewish bands (*klezmer kapella*) were replaced by brass bands as a symbol of the new Soviet militarized reality.

The opportunity for the so-called brotherly peoples to become members of a united Soviet family was rather limited. This did not reflect the truly wide variety of nations in the country—it is sufficient to mention the folklore of Soviet Germans or Soviet Finns, Kalmyks, Crimean Tartars, and Jews, also considered to be outsiders. The world of Jewish music was viewed as representing a miserable group of outcasts who were completely banned shortly after the revolution of 1917. Jewish music was regarded by the Soviet regime to be as dangerous as Hebraic letters, and was considered as revolting to Soviet officials as the smell of incense is to the devil. Jewish elements were banned, although they were used by composers who were not Jews. One example, before World War II, is "The Jewish Overture" by Sergei Prokofiyev and, another, after World War II, is "From Jewish Folk Poetry," the vocal cycle by Dmitry Shostakovich. In the world of Jewish music, a paradoxical thing happened from which we can learn a lesson. We are referring to the fact that the Stalinist officialdom blundered both in banning musical works and in permitting them, and, willingly or unwillingly, many Soviet composers made good use of the political leaders' ignorance and stupidity. The reason was that, unlike words, music could not be labeled in ideological terms although, as we know, music can also be subject to dangerous manipulation. But sometimes it is very difficult to discover a composer's real intent even when the melody can be easily associated with a well-known text. In general, music has so many possible meanings and can be interpreted in so many ways that even the strictest censor can be deceived. For example, although it was banned in Soviet operas, symphonies, and chamber music, Jewish musical intonation passed unnoticed in Soviet mass songs, the most popular genre of our songwriters throughout the nation—the very genre where it would be considered most dangerous from the point of view of the censors. Many people were taken by the melodies in songs composed by Isaac Dunayevsky, the Pokrass brothers, Matvey Blanter, and by other Jewish and sometimes even non-Jewish composers whose works enjoyed popularity in the country. One case in point involves the choral work "Song about Stalin," which was performed throughout the whole Soviet Union—especially by all the finest State Russian Choirs—as a popular Russian folksong of the new era (anonymous, of course!), but was created by the Jewish composer Victor Belyj (1904–1983). Once again, we owe our knowledge of this fact to Professor Yevgeny Hippius who was a close friend, neighbor, and even contemporary of the composer. Thinking about Jewish music in the USSR, we say: love does find a way!

As for Russian folklore, the situation was especially complex because of the two-faced policies of the Soviet regime. In part this was recently described by Victor Lapin in his 1991 article, "The Destruction of Folklore and Ecology of Culture." A few important articles about the real history of Russian folkloristics can be found in the new Russian journal *Zhivaya Starina* (Living Antiquity), which first appeared in 1994. A truthful account of the Russian people's reaction to Party control over folklore was published by Elena Razumovskaya in the 1991 issue of *Zvenya* (Links). Her paper "Sixty Years of Kolkhoz Life in the Eyes of the Peasants," contains statements and songs by people well versed in the Russian oral tradition. One of them remarked bitterly, "The government did not want our songs." Another person quoted in the paper recalls an episode from the late 1940s, when an official from the regional center came to his village to address a meeting and declared that folk music was "backward," and that new Soviet songs and marches should be sung "in order to inspire the population." In the 1940s, too, a campaign was launched against prominent professionals in many fields. The ominous term "bourgeois scholarship" was invented and put into circulation. Academics' contacts with foreign colleagues were abruptly interrupted. The followers of Nikolay Marr, comparativists, and so-called cosmopolitans (i.e., Jews, according to Soviet terminology) were ruthlessly denounced and expelled from their universities, institutions, conservatories, or colleges. We will name but a few: Victor Zhirmunsky, Mark Azadovsky, Vladimir Propp, Lidiya Kershner (Izaly Zemtsovsky's first mentor in ethnomusicology).

The situation in regard to academic scholarship was so bitter that, we reluctantly recall a sorrowful slogan in Russia: "If you don't adapt you kick the bucket; if you don't kick the bucket, you'll adapt!" We fervently hope that the true and sometimes enigmatic history of folkloristics and ethnomusicology under the Soviets, with all its unbelievable ups and downs, will be written in the near future on the basis of both state and private archives and testimonies.

Our colleagues in the West must be made aware that they cannot rely upon Soviet folklore publications, since these distort, rather than reflect, the actual state of things. Much of what was published in those years is a falsification. For example, songs about the civil war hero Nikolay Shchors, who was no hero at all, are not true folksongs but were ordered directly by Stalin in 1935 and forced upon people through a widely distributed film about this "hero." (In passing, we should point out that the role of Soviet films in propagandizing new so-called folk and mass songs was enormous and deserves special attention.) A similar situation obtained in regard to numerous publications by Sergey Aksiuk and even with *Modern Siberian Songs*, a totally false book cynically compiled by Valentin Levashov, who for many years was director of the famous Pyatnitsky Choir (this was verified by Professor Yevgeny Hippius and his students; Prof. Hippius communicated his findings personally to Dr. Zemtsovsky).

Because of their immediate response to whatever was going on in both the provinces and the country as a whole, *chastushkas* were also exploited. Their publication was strictly selective. Everything lively, critical, or sarcastic was removed, and these songs were sterilized with respect to politics, sex, or obscenities.[2]

Everything was kept under control: for instance, the outstanding Kazakh *akyn*-improvisor Djambul Djabayev (1846–1945), famous as far back as the beginning of the twentieth century, if not even earlier, created his first song in 1862 and gained nationwide popularity long before Soviet power. In the second half of the 1930s, Djambul had two Russian secretaries appointed to him, who informed him about current events in the light of the so-called "permitted" truth. They sometimes even ordered themes for his beautiful improvisations and then wrote them down with much editing and expurgation, especially for the official Russian translations of his poetry. The Soviets made attempts to tame such gifted poets as *akyn* Djambul, the Lezgin *ashug* Sulejman Stal'skij, and the Tajik traditional poet-performer *hafiz* Lakhuti. Their compositions were translated into other national languages of the USSR and were published individually. All of them were elected to membership in the Writers' Union.

Moldavian songs were expurgated by removing traditional geographical names since they were Rumanian. Izaly Zemtsovsky was offered a commission to write a book on Moldavian-Ukrainian cultural relations with the understanding that he would prove they were more persistent, older, and better than those between Moldavia and Rumania. Had he written the book, he might have been made (for the moment) a hero of the Moldavian Republic. He declined the offer without the slightest hesitation, but the book was written shortly afterwards—by someone else. Another example: Zemtsovsky was not allowed to publish a folksong about the February Revolution of 1917, which was considered a bourgeois revolution, since it was impossible—a priori—for a bourgeois revolution to have a folksong composed about it.

Censorship was terrible: the State fought against folklore by fighting first against folklorists. Involved in the struggle were religious motifs in folklore and in folkloristics. Anti-religious folklore was fabricated (by Victor Sidelnikov and others). There exists a library copy of the book by Yevgeny Trubetskoy on the Russian fairytale, published in 1922, in which the printer had to black out all the lines dealing with Christianity.[3]

Outright bans were frequent, all-embracing, and unpredictable. For example, Azerbaijani singers (*khanende*) were not allowed to perform the traditional *mugam* (the favorite vocal-instrumental genre of Azerbaijan professional music of oral tradition) "Bayaty-Shiraz." They offered, half-jokingly, to alter the name to "Bayaty-Moscow"—but permission was not granted all the same.

But Russian history continues. About ten years ago an official from the All-Russian Ministry of Culture, in all seriousness, formulated the State's position as follows: "The biggest danger (the spread of nationalism) involves your notorious folklore ensembles. It is necessary that the representatives of all Soviet peoples become members of each ensemble!" This sounded strange even at that time, but today we are forced to remember this pathological slogan because of our new "too pure" folklore ensembles, which, in reality, are sometimes based on outspokenly racist principles: for instance, "There is not a single half-breed in our national group!" This is just what is not needed. Russia really is a country of extremes.

Quite recently, a Russian editor removed all instances of the word "Macedonian" from a book on South Slavic epics. Quite naturally, the author of the book took out all mention of the word "Bulgarian." As a result, historical truth was distorted. Another example: in Kazakhstan, local folklore about the Russian Cossack chief Yermak (Zharmak in Kazakh) was banned because, during his conquest of Siberia, he had drowned hundreds of villages along the Irtysh river in blood. The Kazakh avenger Satbek killed Yermak in single combat and became a national hero. Kazakh songs about this legendary battle were forbidden in Soviet times. Forbidden, too, was the folklore of the twelve peoples repressed under Stalin: Germans from the Volga provinces, Tartars from the Crimea, Ingushi, Balkars, Karachays, Kalmyks, Vepsy, and so on.

The Party waged a fierce campaign against old customs and traditions. New socialist festivals and ceremonies were continuously created and forced on people, with accompanying music, songs, and instructions distributed all over the country. The motto was, "new times—new songs—new customs—new traditions—new human beings, the builders of communism." In fact, it was a movement from genuine folklore to, let us say, "trade-union folklore," i.e., a new and artificial tradition organized from above as a means of "improving" the style, texts, melodies, and musical instruments, and aimed toward general unification, control, and administration.

Olga Freidenberg (a St. Petersburg philologist and a cousin of Boris Pasternak) wrote in her memoirs published in the journal *Prometei* that Marxism in the Soviet Union was not an outlook or a method, but a whip "belonging with the punitive organs and the police." It should be admitted, however, that the best Soviet scholars learned the trick of using the protective covering of Marxist-Leninist phraseology to save the main ideas that came to them irrespective of Marxism and, more often than not, despite Marxism. Hence, not all works quoting from the classics of Marxism-Leninism need to be rejected immediately or completely. Scholarly achievement under the Soviet is an important subject and one worthy of special investigation.

We can say for certain that there was no such phenomenon as "Soviet folkloristics," in the sense that it included all of us equally. The unity was geographical rather than ideological. Today, one can describe at least three types of Soviet scholar. One type (such as V. Sidelnikov, S. Vasilenok and, alas, others) was the so-called "blunt informer" who took part in ideological programs in person. A second type (such as Nikolai Babushkin, Vasilii Potiavin, or Nikolai Kravtsov) was the "tireless fighter" for Marxist ideology. A third type (including Mark Azadovsky, Vladimir Propp, Viktor Zhirmunsky, Ivan Tolstoy, and the still-living Eleazar Meletinsky and Boris Putilov) consisted of great, original scholars whose works are worthy of study. Of course, the stamp of time has touched them all differently. Even in the 1920s and 1930s, for instance, when Soviet folkloristics openly rejected the anthropological (or as we called it, the "ethnographic") approach to folklore research and proclaimed that folklore was nothing but verbal art and should be investigated as "oral literature," Vladimir Propp studied the historical and ethnographic roots of magic tales, while later, Vladimir Chicherov studied calendar songs both as a philologist and as an ethnographer. There are indeed no rules without exceptions.

Nonetheless, we know that the consequences of such politics in scholarship were deplorable. Compelled to study folklore only as a verbal art, Soviet folklorists could only use so-called "aesthetic" criteria. The aesthetics of folklore became itself a new and fundamental discipline, full of wearisome theorizing about the "national character" of folklore and its creative method, which in essence should be, of course, realistic, and so on and so forth. The climax of Marxist aesthetics in the USSR was the monograph, *The Aesthetics of Folklore* (1967) by Viktor Gusev, a work loaded with convoluted phraseology, which became almost obligatory in Russia as a model Marxist handbook.

It is of interest to sum up the communist methods of cultural unification with the example of Soviet Central Asia. We will examine the musical policy in the area in general and in Kazakhstan in particular. First of all the oral tradition was, step by step, replaced by a system of state schools. "Orchestras of Folk Instruments" were founded everywhere and these required (an apparently innocent requirement) music-making in unison. This requirement had a revolutionary consequence for the fate of folklore in the region, because Kazakhstan, was traditionally without music-making of this kind; Kazakh musicians never played in unison. Traditional musicians were trained to play in unison and solo performance was replaced by ensembles. After a change of participants, even musical thinking itself (that is, the core of musical tradition in general, its "holy of holies") was irreversibly altered. The boundary between folk and art music (i.e., music of the European type, a written tradition) was eradicated.

In regard to traditional epics, a whole series of attacks began with Stalinist repression of the best epic singers (*zhyrau*) and ended with the imposition of the Russian idea of the heroic folk epic as the only permissible type of epic on the Kazakh narrative tradition, despite their fundamental differences between these two. Naturally after that, false compilations of huge epics began, and the traditional Central Asian talent for improvisation was used at the government's bidding for ideological purposes.

Traditional national song competitions (*aitys)* were banned, and from 1934 through 1980 not a single Kazakh *aitys* took place. Reintroduction of the *aitys* was made in a monstrous fashion: instead of genuine improvisation, all expected dialogues, questions, and answers were created beforehand and were devoted to the realities of Soviet life (e.g., a summons about town-planning in Almaty was answered by rhymes about people who were late to work). In the name of the people, State authorities offered their own decrees, an action which, at the beginning of the 1980s, amused people.

Mass shows were created in Central Asia, modeled after the new, huge, Russian state ensembles. In Kazakhstan, where there were no traditional dances at all, a special new choreographic collective, "The State Ensemble for Song and Dance," was created by the famous dancer known as "Shara," and Kazakh people came to like it. We see how these artificial processes, organized from above, have changed the core of the traditional legacy, i.e., the artistic thinking and cultural perception of the people.

The outstanding Georgian philosopher Merab Mamardashvili coined the aphorism: "Totalitarianism first and foremost is a linguistic suppression." This phrase, which became an axiom for the whole history of the Soviet regime, relates to all kinds of languages, including thoughts about music and music itself. Over and over again we learned "to amuse ourselves within the walls of our prison."

We have already been depraved by the cultural market: we do what they expect to receive from us. In the past "they" were in Moscow, now "they" are located somewhere in the West. The "Iron Curtain" has fallen. "What can we do for you, dear Western customers?" He who pays calls the tune, and today our folklore managers are consumer-oriented. Now, for instance, huge and unwieldy "patriotic choruses" from the Soviet past have gone out of fashion because their old customers have disappeared; instead, we offer today our "most archaic rituals," our "most authentic shamans" and so on in the latest fashion. One could say that a commercial Satan runs the show. As a result, the artificial has become natural. We learned to be fond of a "new folklore tradition" with new forms and we juggled a content that in the past had been unbearably false.

We have been converted to the new era. We have become "the others." We are human beings at the crossroads, i.e., in-between—perhaps between *homo sovieticus* and *homo eurasiaticus* en route to the *human being who has freely discovered himself*? All this is still unknown, but it seems the Russia of old no longer exists. There remain only the horrible and uneradicated consequences of our tragic Soviet past. For the time being our true culture is concealing itself. Who knows how fast this change will increase, without being new?

In post-communist Russia and in the Commonwealth of Independent States (CIS), the most prominent forms of folklore are those that used to be forbidden under Soviet communism. And it is only natural that this should be so. Among the prevailing genres are Soviet political folklore (including jokes and anecdotes, *chastushki,* songs and prose written by the GULAG inmates), horror or terrifying stories and sadistic tales told by children (including short poems), graffiti, scrapbooks of teenagers and young soldiers, prison songs, the singing of camp, underworld, and oral religious poems, religious verses (*dukhovnye stikhi*); and the folklore of several "taboo" groups such as the Crimean Tatars, Volga Germans, and Jews. And once again, there is no balance—the true picture of folklore is distorted—only now the bias is in the other direction. It will take time for things to settle down so that we will be able to generalize from past experience.

It can be readily noticed that the taboo works contain a curious combination of the anti-Soviet (i.e., ideological underground) and erotica, in other words, the formerly banned "low" culture. (The underground literally lies low, while erotica has always been considered low—a traditional view held by many authors, most notably Mikhail Bakhtin.) The carnival side of life was banned, that life which is beyond all forms of control, report, regulation, or management. This is why such a curious combination was driven underground and had to exist secretly. The uncontrollable elements in life, the free play of feelings, were regarded as the enemy's ideology. (The relationship is not unlike that between life and imprisonment: as prison is the enemy of life, so life is the enemy of prison.) This phenomenon explains the current popularity of erotic literature, which is published and republished. This forbidden side of life is freeing itself; the latest publication is the 640-page volume of *Russian Erotic Folklore*, compiled by Andrei Toporkov (Moscow 1995).

In conclusion, we will make a general statement from the cases and facts relevant to the pre-*perestroika* era of Soviet folklore and folkloristics. As ophthalmologist Svyatoslav Fedorov put it, "Since 1917, our country has been trying to appear a civilized state whereas it has always been one huge concentration camp." These words make one understand the reasons for such the wide popularity in the USSR of thieves' songs—songs making use of thieves' jargon, a hoarse voice, and specific manner of performance (which is also true of some songs by Vladimir Vysotsky, the extremely popular Russian artist and so-called "guitar bard"). The answer to the question "why?" is self-evident: consciously or subconsciously, we all felt ourselves prisoners. The songs were a small breakthrough to freedom. They spoke our thoughts, they were the resounding trumpet and the poetry that could not be subjugated by any authority.

The situation can be understood from a Soviet Jewish anecdote (for us, it is the best folk symbol of the Soviet GULAG of a country): two Jews share a cell in prison; one asks the other, "Look here, Avromele, why are the prison bars so strong? Do they think anyone will take it into their head to try and get in here?"

Notes
[1] These are some of the titles made known to the public in the last thirty years (meaning after the death of Stalin!): *Lenin's Work "Materialism and Empiriocriticism' and the Problem of Folkloristics* by Vasily Potyavin (1961), *On the Marxist-Leninist Basis for the Theory of People's Poetic Creativity* by Nikolay Babushkin (1965), *The Role of Folklore in Communist Education* by Lazare Eliasov (1967), *Artistic Creativity of the Masses under Socialism* by Fedor Prokofyev (1978), *World-Outlook and Soviet Folklore* by Anton Petrukhin (1983), *The Ideological Function of Music* by Igor Nabok (1987);*The All-Union Inter-Ethnical System of Spiritual Culture in the Light of the Resolution Adopted by the 27th Congress of CPSU* by Victor Sherstobitov (1987).
[2] A brave exception in 1968 was Yuri Burtin's paper on *chastushkas,* which was published in the monthly magazine *Novy Mir [New World]*, No. 1; see also *Zhivaya Starina* (1994, No. 2) on the archives of Alexander Nikiforov (1893–1942).
[3] In regard to Islam under the Soviets, see the book, *Mystics and Commissars*, by Alexandre Bennigsen and S. Enders Wimbush, University of California Press, 1985.

BARBARA KIRSHENBLATT-GIMBLETT

Is Folklore Ever Innocent?

The destruction of cultural forms under the pretext of preservation, while it took particularly reprehensible forms in the USSR, has precedents in the Protestant Reformation, the French Revolution, the formation of colonial empires, the emergence of nation states, and the reform of Judaism in the nineteenth century, to mention some of the more obvious cases. Utopian longings notwithstanding, the world imagined under the banner of folklore is a battlefield. Which is not to say that all combat waged there is equally bloody, or that the terms of the conflict are the same. What distinguishes the USSR, in the account provided by Izaly Zemtsovsky and Alma Kunanbaeva, is the historic location of the process and the particular forms that it took.

Though it is tempting to think that folklore exists prior to its study, the history of the category is not the same as the history of that which the category comes to cover. Furthermore, the category itself has agency, for good and for bad. This agency is at the heart of what Zemtsovsky and Kunanbaeva describe in their account of folklore in the Soviet Union.

"Communism and Folklore" exposes the worst abuses of totalitarianism made in the name of folklore. This paper also suggests parallels with other efforts to suppress popular traditions, "to destroy folklore under the pretext of its preservation," to fabricate and promulgate traditions by force, and to resist all such efforts. Whatever the parallels, however, these processes play themselves out in historically and culturally specific ways. Aware of the already political nature of folklore as a category and field of study—of their agency—the Soviets did not eliminate them. Rather they redirected them to serve their objectives. The brutality of the process is consistent with the methods of totalitarian regimes.

Richard M. Dorson's distinction between folklore and fakelore obscures these issues, though we can appreciate why he would insist on lambasting fakelore given his efforts to establish folklore as a legitimate field of study in the academy. The notion of the "invention of tradition" put forward by Eric Hobsbawm and Terence Ranger in the collection of essays they edited turns the table, by suggesting how extensively traditions are invented, programmatically and out of whole cloth, while claiming otherwise. These themes are also taken up by Hermann Bausinger in his pathbreaking book, *Folk Culture in a World of Technology* (1990[1961]),

Tamas Hofer in his analysis of the folk cultural heritage and Hungarian national identity (1989), William Rowe and Vivian Schelling in their account of popular culture in Latin America (1991), and Johannes Fabian (1990) in his notion of folklore as a mode of production.

Long processes of "cultural evolution," violent revolutions, and systematic programs of reform leave behind what they have rejected. Through a process of archaizing, which is a mode of cultural production, the repudiated is transvalued as folklore. The Protestant Reformation played an instrumental role in dividing the domain of what we think of as culture into its preferred and despised categories. Catholic Europe became a source of fascination for Protestants eager to see what the Reformation had opposed.

Just how reform works to create the domain of the popular can be seen in *Popular Culture and Elite Culture in France, 1400–1750* (1985: 1). Defining popular culture as "one of history's losers," Robert Muchembled sets out to prove that "popular culture does exist," despite attempts to repress it, including its absence in the historical record. While Muchembled is arguing for the existence of popular culture, I am suggesting that whatever practices he may identify with it, the category "popular culture" is itself an historical formation coincident with the repressions he describes. By examining the "archeology of centralizing power" (p. 312), whether that power be in the hands of the church or the state, Muchembled's study of popular culture shows that repression in the name of reform has a long history and that popular culture has long provided an arena for the struggle.

Paradoxically, remembering is a prelude to forgetting and the collecting of error a prelude to its eradication. The history of the study of popular antiquities is driven by precisely this principle, as the title of Sir Thomas Browne's *Enquiries into Vulgar and Common Errors* (1649) suggests (p. 52). Steven Mullaney (1983) provides a particularly vivid example of this principle at work. During the royal entry into Rouen of Henry II in 1550, Brazilian villages stocked with Native Americans for the occasion and supplemented with Frenchmen in military attire, was the scene of a mock siege and French triumph. Mullaney's analysis focuses not so much on the recreation of this event as on its erasure: "The ethnographic attention and knowledge displayed at Rouen was genuine, amazingly thorough, and richly detailed; the object, however, was not to understand Brazilian culture but to perform it, in a paradoxically self-consuming fashion" (p. 48). He argues further that the interest in Brazilian culture displayed at Rouen served "ritual rather than ethnological ends, and the rite involved is one ultimately organized around the elimination of its own pretext" (p. 48). Such performances, he continues, are rehearsals, in the legal sense of the term, and are to be understood within a dramaturgy of power that first exhibits what it "consigns to oblivion" (pp. 49, 52).

As Mona Ozouf demonstrates in her landmark book, *Festivals and the French Revolution* (1988), the Revolution entailed not only the rejection of the old cultural order, but also the systematic creation of a regime of social experience in which new forms of festivity were to play a central role in educating and transforming the citizenry. This process produced what Ozouf calls a "shameful ethnology" (p. 218). An instrument of the Revolution's "repressive militantism" (p. 223), negative accounts of traditional practices measured the success of the Revolution in eradicating what it repudiated and the rebellious potential of what persisted.

The process of negating cultural practices reverses itself once it has succeeded in archaizing the "errors." The very term "folklore" marks a transformation of errors into archaisms and their transvaluation once they are safe for collection, preservation, exhibition, study, and even nostalgia and revival. In England, where the term folklore was coined in 1846, it referred to "survivals" in a civilized society of behaviors that had their origins in earlier stages of cultural evolution. On the continent, the term or its rough equivalents (*Volkskunde, traditions populaires*) referred to the purity of national culture preserved in rural backwaters outside the cosmopolitanizing reach of the metropole.

The Jewish case is instructive. The attempt to reform Jewish life by repudiating customary practices created a large domain of cultural trash, which returned decades later as "folklore." During the early nineteenth century, *Sulamit*, a popular little magazine in German for Jewish readers, ran a column entitled "Gallery of Obnoxious Abuses, Shocking Customs, and Absurd Ceremonies of the Jews," a mode of writing I call the ethnographic burlesque. The author, David Fraenkel, first contrasts the simplicity and naturalness of life in the Bible with the bizarre ceremonialism introduced by the rabbis. He then urges readers to adopt the aesthetic and refined manner of cosmopolitan Jews. In an account of wedding customs, for example, the author objects to matchmaking because it seems to ignore the desires of the young couple and focus on crass financial transactions. The author questions the use of an incomprehensible language, Hebrew-Aramaic, for something as important as the marriage ceremony. He is offended by the public spectacle of outdoor processions accompanied by music because the bridal couple is put on public display in a filthy courtyard. What is worse, such ridiculous wedding customs look like fools play to the non-Jews. How much preferable are the refined practices of the Jews in Leipzig who hold their wedding ceremonies discreetly in the nicest room in the city.

Such descriptions oppose traditional practices to the bourgeois ideals that are considered prerequisites for the social integration of Jews. Reform is here promulgated not at gun point but through a process illuminated by Norbert Elias's notion of "What may be described as an advance of the threshold of embarrassment and shame, as 'refinement,' or as 'civilization'" (Elias 1982:101). The ethnographic burlesque induces shame at thresholds of its own making. This art of rhetorically induced estrangement mobilizes the will of the reader to abandon established custom and internalize new forms of sensibility and conduct. In this way, cultural inscription prepares the ground for change.

In the process, ethnographic burlesque also enlarges the terrain of ethnography. By narrowing the domain of what could be considered normative, critics of traditional ceremonies and customs simultaneously expanded the field of the non-normative, which was to become the heart-land of ethnographic investigation. What one was too ashamed to do, one could study. Fifty years later, the vituperation we see in Sulamit would give way to nostalgia and the very wedding customs that Fraenkel burlesqued would be offered by Joseph Perles as a critique of Jewish respectability (see Kirshenblatt-Gimblett 1990).

To the extent that folklore can be understood as a mode of cultural production, the Soviets attacked the archaizing tendencies of the old category. They repressed earlier content, its positive identification with ways of life they repudiated, and the ideological content of the category. In its stead, they promulgated folklore as a mode of contemporary, if not futuristic, cultural production consistent with the ideology and objectives of the Soviet state. What could not be found was to be fabricated—program-matically, systematically, on pain of death. This is not to suggest that there are only two approaches—archaism and imposed fabrication—but only to complicate the Soviet story by suggesting the agency of the category of folklore. There is on the one hand the claimed neutrality of Western science, upheld as free of political entanglement. There is on the other hand activist or engaged scholarship, born of principled commitments. What "Commu-nism and Folklore" demonstrates is the degree to which the Soviet regime debased the latter in the name of the former, on the strength of the agency of folklore.

MARK SLOBIN

Thoughts on Zemtsovsky's and Kunanbaeva's "Communism and Folklore"

Izaly Zemtsovsky and Alma Kunanbaeva, from their excellent vantage point as insiders, raise salient issues and tell fascinating tales about the history of folklore studies in the Soviet Union. In response, I would like to add a couple of brushstrokes to their broad canvas from the point of view of an outside observer who made several trips to the USSR from 1968–1990.

The first point I would like to make concerns the local vs. the national, (or the "all-Union," as it used to be called) in Soviet ethnomusicology and folklore studies. Distinctions need to be drawn about varieties of cultural activity under the vast umbrella of official policy. I learned something about this as head of American delegations that met twice with Soviet ethnomusicologists (1988, 1989), once in the USSR and once in the United States, under the auspices of the International Research and Exchanges Board (IREX). I noticed distinctive attitudes towards theory and method that cropped up among the Soviet delegation, and questioned the participants, who readily admitted the strong regional divisions in scholarly orientation that existed behind the facade of dictated policy. For example, the Baltic states of Estonia, Latvia, and Lithuania retained strong intellectual ties to the Germanic school of folklore studies, while Russian scholars were more apt to be influenced by the work of Boris Asaf'iev, the great twentieth-century Russian music theorist. Central Asians, while strongly under the spell of Russian theory and methodology, nevertheless had their kinship to Middle Eastern and Indian sources and practice always in the back of their minds, moving to the foreground more openly as things opened up with the progressive indigenization of scholarship in the 1970s.

Similar distinctions in implicit and explicit models for research existed at even more local levels, such as the difference between the training and approach of Russian scholars from Moscow and Leningrad (the once and future St. Petersburg), based partly on pre-Revolutionary patterns. Within the "Transcaucasus" zone, the republics of Armenia, Georgia, and Azerbaijan had quite individual role models and outlooks of scholarship that articulated and inflected the way they responded to the "social command" policies directed by the all-Union organs of culture.

Locally, as we have come to learn, non-scholarly activists used the very structures of cultural bureaucracy, like the House of Culture, to support as well as distort folklore repertoires, traditions, and attitudes. As elsewhere, the nation-state's intrusion into local life was complex, sometimes contradictory, and always somewhat uneven, allowing for certain spaces of non-normative behavior to open up. Thus, in terms of both local approaches and local responses, an eventual history of Soviet folkloristics (which should certainly be undertaken) would want to spread a set of transparent overlays over the general map laid out by Zemtsovsky and Kunanbaeva.

It is also important to remember that locally, scholars kept on doing traditional pre-Soviet folklore research in many places. This does not mean they could openly support older, no longer acceptable forms of folklore or publish what they knew, but they could maintain the trust and confidence of their rural informants without sacrificing their integrity as scholars/citizens, waiting for a change of the political weather to make their research known. Those ethnomusicologists and folklorists who did stay the course deserve special recognition; it would be gratuitous to single out individuals here, of course, but appropriate to mention Zemtsovsky and Kunanbaeva as two such scholars.

A second, larger point that occurs to me in response to their essay is the need to distinguish "socialist" folkloristics from the general pattern of modern folklore studies in general. Many of the shortcomings of Soviet policies are merely part of an overall thrust of culture and society in the USSR that can be read as an exaggeration of tendencies found across Europe and the United States as part of the project we call "modernity." The idea of the state being charged with subsidizing the collection, publication, and performance of folklore, for example, has been widespread in Euro-America for generations. Specific attitudes towards folklore e.g., prudishness, are not just Soviet. The great Anglo-American scholars were just as eager to keep "crude" lyrics and topics out of their anthologies as were Soviet policymakers. One thinks of the eminent American folklorist Vance Randolph, waiting until he was nearly ninety to publish the scatological and erotic materials from the Ozark mountains that he had collected decades earlier.

More significantly, the manipulation and re-creation of folklore—the "fakelore" issue—was hardly restricted to the Soviet Union. The African slave narratives collected under government-sponsored programs of the 1930s in the United States were edited to portray a uniform "slave" speech regardless of whether the informants spoke "correct" or various dialect forms of English. It is rumored that the canonical versions of some

African American songs on archival recordings were partly influenced by suggestions made by collectors for the sake of "authenticity." Indeed, in various Euro-American traditions, the "folk" themselves have been the most energetic in "setting standards" and arbitrarily conferring legitimation upon performers, repertoire, and style.

The issue, then, is not just to point out that Soviet folkloristics "distorted" a presumed "genuine" folklore, but to identify the existence of specific mechanisms that marked the Soviet system off from a general, modern Euro-American approach to folklore studies. As Zemtsovsky and Kunanbaeva point out, the backdrop of brutal repression was probably the most obvious distinctive feature of the USSR's daily practice. Western societies had more subtle and less pervasive methods of control underlying the everyday implementation of acceptable folklore norms. The specter of state-sponsored terror was part of a generally much more intrusive layer of bureaucracy that spread across a vast and culturally heterogeneous landscape. Similarly, rewards were proportionately greater for proper behavior, both on the part of informants and folklorists, in terms of public recognition, medals, access to privileges, and the like.

The gradual spread throughout the late 1920s and 1930s of this inexorable bureaucratization of folklore had significant, purely Soviet consequences. While homogenization of folklore occurred all across Euro-America in a variety of ways, within the USSR, systems of representation and repression tended to exaggerate this process. While taking part in the American delegation to the Second (and final) Soviet-sponsored International Folklore Festival, held in Kiev in 1990, I could see for myself the results of this approach. Each delegation, either from a Soviet political subdivision (Autonomous Republic, Republic) or a visiting foreign-country participant, was assigned a costumed, placard-holding maiden identifying the group, and each group was expected to file down the main street of the city from the entrance of one soccer stadium to the inside of another. Once in the stadium, all delegations circulated around the track while a chosen crowd used flashcards and cheers to greet participants. This sort of "normal" presentation of folklore had an intensely homogenizing effect rendered all the more visible by the beginnings of dissidence shown by individual delegations in subtle ways at this late moment in Soviet official folklore; a year later, the USSR had ceased to exist. Richard Kurin (1992), the head of the American delegation, has written an insightful essay detailing the Soviet position and American disagreements that sparked a lively debate at that 1990 Festival. His own position as bureaucrat, for the Smithsonian Institution, however modestly and democratically, presupposes notions of state-supported "preservation" and encouragement of local "heritages" as part of modernity's rationalization of culture. Even within American intellectual circles there has been a substantial critique of local and national folklore festivals. The difference, as I've suggested, lies in the harshness and the pervasiveness of the penetration of tradition and particularly of scholarship in the Soviet world, which represented modernity to the maximum.

Finally, Zemtsovsky and Kunanbaeva quite reasonably stay within the bounds of the Soviet experience in critiquing "socialist" and "communist" folkloristics. The comparative study of the situation of all "socialist" states has only recently begun, but is essential in understanding what happened in the USSR. Not only eastern, central, and southeastern Europe, but China, North Korea, Vietnam, Cuba, and African Marxist-leaning states need to be looked at as experiments in state-controlled culture for us to understand how the Soviet Union, as both initial experiment and eventual model, functioned as a laboratory of totalitarian folkloristics. Here the question of "local" vs. Soviet is projected across a global landscape of overarching ideology and on-the-ground modification, domestication, and continual redefinition of goals, methods, and achievements. Even under "postcommunism," national dance troupes flourish everywhere, traditions are reinvented and nationalized by bureaucrats, and folklorists have a hard time working outside the immediate political pressures of funding agencies or other vested sources of patronage. In the final analysis, what we need to learn from the Soviet experience is not so much the terrible waste of careers and the deformation of scholarship, but the steadiness and courage of researchers who strove to maintain an internal intellectual and moral independence against the invasive, consciousness-bending forces of imposed systems of thought and mechanisms of repression.

IRINA GUTKIN

The Historical Paradoxes of Soviet Folklore and Folkloristics: A Response to Zemtsovsky and Kunanbaeva

The sorrowful, and at times tragic, story of folklore and folkloristics under the Soviet regime presented by Drs. Zemtsovsky and Kunanbaeva paradoxically attests to the fact that the strength of "the only true scientific teaching" (which Marxism-*cum*-Leninism, -Stalinism, and -Brezhnevism proclaimed themselves to be) was precisely its ability to prevent the construction of alternative ideologies that in a pluralistic society normally co-exist in competition. Hence, like a deceased ancestor in a pre-modern society, this dead Soviet ideology still commands undivided attention from the grave: in its formidable all-encompassing totality, its seductive doctrine still holds sway over post-Soviet culture, as its ideology has thus far remained that principal ideological "other" with which this culture is now waging a dialogic battle.

It has been observed that throughout its history, Russian culture preferred revolution—a violently radical rejection of the preceding tradition—over evolution. Indeed, the initial reaction of post-Soviet culture was to reverse all former Soviet oppressive hierarchies by simply turning them upside down. In a rush to replace the mythic Soviet pantheon, new martyrologies have been hastily created on the principle that everything that used to be repressed must now be eulogized. In the field of folkloristics this trend is manifest in the prevailing interest in "unofficial" folklore, especially that of the GULAG. (Another fashionable genre in post-Soviet folkloristics is the so-called "anecdotes," or jokes, from political types to those of children's black humor.)

Such practices are a sure indication that the Soviet past has not as yet become history proper. Likewise, the necessary analytical detachment that comes with a self-conscious awareness of the epistemological problems involved in a given methodology and of one's own ideological inclinations—the *sine qua non* of the present-day post-Foucaultian research in the humanities in the West—has not as yet become the intellectual habit of post-Soviet scholars. Hence, the academic forums of the post-Soviet era tend to turn into therapeutic outlets for a culture in need of healing, whereby emotionally wrenching revelations and denunciations of the atrocities of the fallen regime are intermingled with a touch of *mea culpa*. It was heartening, however, to hear Dr. Zemtsovsky's acknowledgment that in post-Soviet folkloristics "there is a bias in the other direction and it will take time for things to settle down so that we would be able to generalize."

In order for Soviet folkloristics to become history, historically nuanced accounts of the function and fate of folklore in Soviet culture need to be produced. Since under the Soviet system folklore was used in ways markedly different from those typical to both traditional pre-modern communities and in Western industrialized societies (but also different from other "totalitarian" societies such as Nazi Germany), a better under-standing of the specific nature and function of folklore in Soviet culture can be reached if it is viewed with regard to the inherent logic informing that culture.

The history of Soviet folklore should not be construed entirely in an elegiac or tragic mode. A focus on the difficult fate of the so-called "unofficial folklore" should not eclipse the fact that the Soviet State gave generous support to folklore studies. Surely, this support fed an army of academic opportunists who occupied themselves with politically correct, if also safely jejeune, topics. However, it also provided for the expeditions of the Sokolov brothers, A.M. Astakhova, M. K. Azadovsky and scores of other scholars to record folk traditions in the Russian North; all other parts of the enormous Soviet empire received comparable attention. The results of this work will provide employment for generations of scholars, both in Russia and the West. Furthermore, in spite of the ideological "categorical imperative," in many officially sanctioned areas Soviet folklorists pro-duced generally solid, and in some cases, impressive scholarship, just as their Western counterparts had.

Nor can it be assumed that uses of folklore during the Soviet period were subject to some unchanging "official" policy prescribed by the Party. As the character of the Soviet utopia in the 1920s was different from that which predominated in the Stalinist 1930s, so were the culture's attitudes toward folklore at different stages of Soviet history. Embarking as they did on their "grandiose experiment," the Bolshevik leadership did not have much of a practical program for any aspect of the project save the politics of seizing power; the creation of "new culture" was its least theorized part. The Bolshevik leaders, notably Lenin, harbored suspicion of "popular" tastes and conceived of the new socialist culture as vaguely based upon pre-existing historical "high" culture (Howell 1994: 79). Initially they were apparently wary of the use of traditional folk rituals for propaganda purposes since, on the one hand, this idea had its origin in the theories of

Alexander Bogdanov (a one-time Bolshevik whom Lenin considered an idealist, heretic, and political enemy) which likened art to religion as a force able to connect phenomena and ideas on a supra-rational level and thus to "organize" human activity. On the other hand, using folk forms would in the Bolshevik view constitute promotion of that peasant culture which the Bolsheviks associated with Russia's deeply ingrained "Asiatic" traits, i.e., with the backward, un-European, inefficient, non-industrialized Russia, to which Marxist theory hardly seemed applicable.

As the Russian revolution went on to devour its own children, Bogdanov's theory met a fate similar to other ideas that were initially anathematized as heretical (e.g., Trotsky's industrialization); its heretical origins were conveniently forgotten and it was supplanted by the idea that a new culture can be built by filling old forms with new socialist content. In the first decade after the Revolution, the Sovietization of folklore took the form of diverse spontaneous efforts to supplant the traditional cultural-religious rituals with new Soviet ones. Hence, the ritual of *oktiabriny* (christening and name-day parties in the spirit of the October Revolution), the "Komsomol Christmas," and *chastushki* glorifying the Red Army and disparaging its enemies. (On the use of folk theater in Bolshevik festivals see Chapter 4 of von Geldern 1993.)

By the early 1930s concerted efforts were made "to extricate the popular [culture] from its archaic connotations" (Robin 1990: 18). Thus the peculiar phenomenon of specifically Soviet "folklore" was born through the grafting of new ideological content on to traditional folk forms. Examples of folk genres adapted to the purposes of the Soviet state included *chastushki* —"four-line rhymed ditties used to whip up enthusiasm for government projects" (Oinas 1985: 141)—and the *bylina*; the epic forms of non-Russian folk traditions were put to similar use. New "folk" genres were created—namely, the *novina,* a neo-epic based on the formulaic prosody and imagery of the traditional Russian epic; *skazy,* biographical accounts of remarkable people told by folk narrators; and the notorious letter-poems addressed to Stalin which were "drafted jointly by folk performers and professional poets...[and] were amended at successive mass meetings. After the final version was adopted, it was sent to Stalin, accompanied by tens of thousands (in some cases even several millions) of signatures" (Oinas 1985:141). All these phenomena belonged specifically to the Stalinist era (more precisely, to the 1930s), virtually disappearing in the post-Stalin period.

The doctrinal "general line" of communist construction that was codified under Stalin in effect prescribed the advent of communism as a result of an orderly, planned homogenization of all aspects of life in the Soviet empire, not excepting its multi-national folklore. In practice, the maintenance of the status quo became the principal preoccupation of the Soviet regime. For folklore this meant, for instance, an eventual codification of the repertoire of folk ensembles; changes had to be cleared with special Party/State committees that oversaw the work of such State-subsidized folk performing groups. Dr. Kunanbaeva has stories to tell from the Brezhnev years (otherwise known as the "stagnation period"), of how the wardrobes of a large folk ensemble had to be remade because of the color-code system imposed from above for national ensembles: the Kazakh performers had to be dressed in yellow and not green since the latter color was assigned to Kirghizia (or was it the other way around?).

Now let us turn to considerations of theory and methodology vis-à-vis Soviet folklore and folkloristics. To take issue with Dr. Zemtsovsky's generalizing statement that "in brief, folklore was generally replaced with fakelore," it must be said that scholars in the West were equally, if not indeed more aware of the ways in which Soviet folklore was doctored (Oinas 1975; 1976; Howell 1994). Thomas Winner touched upon these problems in his book on the oral art of the Kazakh people when he wrote, with regard to the renowned Kazakh *akyn*, Dzhambul Dzhabaev (1846?–1945), mentioned by Dr. Zemtsovsky: "[T]his celebrated Soviet *akyn* can probably best serve as an example of the difficulties encountered by the researcher, whose material is limited to published Soviet sources, in any attempt at arriving at a sober and objective viewpoint concerning the spontaneity of these modern oral creations and the application of the term 'popular' to them" (Winner 1958: 158).

It is certainly true that much Soviet folklore cannot be expected to meet the principal criteria of authenticity that are applied to traditional folklore—namely those of orality, spontaneity, improvization and anonymity. In Soviet folklore genres, such as the neo-epics, it is impossible to distinguish the hand of the folksingers from that of the folklorists who aided the performers by "improving" their creations. As evidence of the extent to which such interference took place, we have the testimony of Viktorin Popov, the tutor and editor (and it is rumored, one-time lover) of Marfa Kriukova (1876-1954), a gifted performer of epics and laments from the Russian North and perhaps the best-known singer of *noviny,* whom Popov accompanied on her tours of the Soviet Union: "My part in the transcription and revision of the actual legends has been limited to helping her to place certain events in their correct historical sequence; to eliminate abstractions which have no relation to the basic theme; to the considerable curtailment of superfluous repetitions and of descriptions which at certain points were too long and drawn out and which created a disproportion among different parts of the work; and to the elimination of the peculiarities of the White Sea dialect" (cited in Miller 1990: 21). The unabashed forthrightness of Popov's account bespeaks first of all an unwavering conviction in the correctness of this method.

Many concepts and practices of the Soviet folklorists, particularly in early Soviet period, were subsumed by the overarching dogma of the Soviet culture—namely, by the belief that the Bright Future will constitute a perfect synthesis of all historical oppositions, including those between industrialized and rural communities, national entities, manual and intellectual labor, "high" and "popular" culture, and oral and literary poets. Of course, in making this future synthesis, Soviet culture privileged the written word. Sustained efforts were therefore made to educate folk singers. The fact that many singers of epics, especially ethnic Russians, were literate, wrote down their works and then memorized them, was accepted as a desirable or "progressive" manifestation of the "natural" historical process. Some folklorists theorized that the so-called "self-transcribed" method—when the text was written down "at the moment of origin" by the performers themselves—was proof that Soviet folklore had "surpassed the stage" of oral transmission.

Nevertheless, there were divisions among Soviet folklorists in their attitude toward the methods of recording and publishing folkloric texts. Interestingly enough, their theoretical debates often revolved, though not always explicitly, around the problem of "authorship" or "individuality" versus "collectivity" in folklore. In the Soviet context, this perennial problem of folklore theory was colored by the unresolved Marxist dilemma concerning the makers of history—the prominent individuals or the toiling masses. On the one hand, much attention was given to the individual style of gifted perfomers whose work was issued in separate editions. On the other, some folklorists advocated the need to homogenize the language of folklore texts by ridding them of dialectisms and other linguistic idiosyncracies on the grounds that, under Soviet conditions, folklore disseminated in print had to be accessible to large semi-literary and multi-national audiences.

The heated polemics (concerning falsification in the new folklore) that were conducted in print in the late 1930s reveal ambiguities of theory on the part of professional Soviet folklorists. The position of Yuri Sokolov is exemplary of this confusion: Sokolov railed against the many "horrifying falsifications of the traditional and Soviet folklore of both Russian and other national republics of the Soviet Union" as well as against "the irresponsible popularization of folklore, or that which purports to be folklore, on the stage, screen, and radio" (cited in Miller 1990: 22). Yet he classified as falsifications primarily the crude reworkings of folk texts by writers and scholars (e.g., the Soviet version of the Red Riding Hood tale in which the wolf was a *kulak,* and the young girl a *Komsomolka),* and defended, however sincerely, the sanitizing editorial help given to the performers by folklorists and writers such as the aforementioned V. Popov (Miller 1990: 22).

Such Soviet "bowdlerizing" practices are rightly abhorred by today's folklorists. Still, the application of Richard Dorson's time-honored punning distinction ("fakelore") does not help to resolve the epistemological problems concerning the validity of these peculiarly Soviet genres and practices as folk tradition. It is good to keep in mind that our standards and methods are ideational constructs and are subject to historical change. For example, in compiling his famous collection of Russian folk tales, the venerable nineteenth-century Russian folklorist A. N. Afanas'ev (1826-1871) had no qualms about collating versions of a tale recorded from different narrators in order to construct a "comprehensive" text. Our own evalution of authenticity, as with any theoretical construct, is not free from bias.

There is also the open question of "social pressures" experienced by the folk performers. The very circumstances under which the Soviet folk epics were created remain uncertain. Were Dzhambul's poems on Soviet themes merely ascribed to him in print but in fact penned by an "entire brigade of Russian poetasters," as Volkov suggests in his "memoirs" of Dmitrii Shostakovich? (Volkov 1984: 209-210). What was the contribution of the two Russian-speaking "personal secretaries" appointed to the *akyn?* Were they merely a pair of ideological Muses providing the bard with politically correct inspiration, or did they also serve as translators and editors? There is, however, one thing on which the various stories about Dzhambul agree---the notable fact that he was a great folksinger; and this is precisely what makes such questions matter.

Did these folk talents really have to be coerced to compose, in some cases even "at gunpoint" as Dr. Zemtsovky told us? (The story related by late Evgenii Gippius can hardly account for such a widespread participation of singers from diverse languages and traditions). Perhaps a great number of exceptionally talented singers of tales who could improvise a few hundred lines at a stretch were compelled to perform for more universal reasons, such as performer's artistic pride. Are folk singers free from the thrill of stage success, especially once they depart from the traditional context and acquire a taste for it? Talented folk artists enjoyed a most privileged status in the Soviet culture, comparable to that of the Soviet artistic elite. They performed for large audiences; their "concerts" were broadcast over the radio; their work was printed in large editions. Workshops were organized to aid in their ideological reeducation and political awareness; they were honored at special conferences and national and regional competitions. Many became full-fledged members of the Union of Soviet Writers and enjoyed all the privileges that came with the membership. For example, Marfa Kriukova travelled to Stalin's birthplace in the Caucasus, and a fantastic house (*terem*), in pseudo-Russian medieval style was built for her on the shores of the White Sea.

What do we have on record that could help us understand, from the singers' point of view, why they became, as it were, the instruments of Soviet propaganda? How did they feel about putting their talents to ideological use? Did some of them try to find a new arena for their talents because they sensed that the people's interest in traditional folklore was declining and that "they no longer commanded the esteem in their villages that...they had in the past"—a fact that many Soviet folklorists noted at the time? (Miller 1990: 6). Did those who were singing the praises of successful collectivization at the time when it bordered on genocide become so far removed from the reality of their native villages? Or were they perhaps seduced by utopian dreams of the imminent advent of the "Bright Future" and hence in their art felt compelled to show not "what is" but "what ought to be"—as did their counterparts, the professional Socialist Realist writers?

The answers to these questions should be sought in historical and culture-specific circumstances, essentially in the ideological interface between the traditional and Soviet belief systems. For example, the traditional "old" Russian epics (*byliny*) glorify Vladimir the Red Sun—a historical figure and the feudal Prince *par excellence*; but unlike the Tartar epics about Khan Edege, these Russian epics were promoted in every possible way. Or, by the same token, why was converting the *mugam* "Baiaty-Shiraz" into "Baiaty-Moscow" deemed unacceptable, while numerous epics performed by singers skilled in composition-in-performance glorifying the Soviet State were greatly encouraged? If, in Dr. Zemtsovsky's words, the Azeri singers proposed this "half-jokingly", what then really led those folk so readily to fill their ancient forms of art with a new ideology alien to the traditional ideals of their communities? Consider also the fact that the practice of Soviet epics seems to have been inaugurated by some Uzbek *bakshi* (singers of epic poetry) who "during the early 1930s...

performed long poems about Lenin, Stalin, the October revolution, collectivization, the success of Soviet cotton farming, and the cultural revolution"
(Miller 1990: 11). Could it be that so many singers from Central Asian
nations readily placed their talents in the service of Soviet power because
in their native traditions they were "court singers" i.e., in the (ideological)
service of the feudal powerlords, and thus traditionally associated themselves with the powers that be?

Ultimately, the Soviet folk epics cannot be approached in absolute
terms of "true" or "fake" lore, because whatever the pressures on the singers
may have been, in most cases they still used the techniques of oral
composition in which they were skilled. Specialized studies of how the
formulaic modes of national folk epics were adapted to Soviet themes could
potentially add to our understanding of these techniques.

The problem of criteria also applies to the genre of the Soviet
chastushka. In the later days of the Soviet regime the *chastushka* thrived
primarily in the milieu of the intelligentsia; it differed in form and function
from the folk genre (e.g., it was not sung), and some had identifiable authors
(e.g., Igor Guberman). With the advent of Gorbachev's *perestroika,* especially after the coup of August, 1991, a number of newspapers (e.g. *Sovetskaia
Rossiia*) began publishing *chastushkas* solicited from readers; it is not clear
whether they were composed or merely recorded by the contributors.
Considering these facts, does this genre constitute a "true" or "fake"
folklore? It would also be interesting to see a thorough analysis of exactly
how and why the "modern Siberian songs were falsified by Valentin
Levashov." The classification of the GULAG folklore, based on the all-
inclusive five categories that embrace everything from verbal culture in all
its variety to body language (endorsed by the conference mentioned by Dr.
Zemtsovsky), left me wondering how yet another existing distinction could
mesh with this taxonomy: namely, beginning with Solzhenitsyn, camp
literature taught us that within the GULAG there were two very distinct
cultures at war with each other—-that of the (organized) criminals, and that
of the political prisoners. Is this split reflected in the body of folklore? Has
this problem been addressed by the conference?

To a present-day student of Soviet folklore it may come as a surprise
that folk "authenticity" of the Sovietized traditional genres could be, and
indeed was, questioned in the Stalinist 1930s (in the "official press") by the
folklorists who earned a reputation as rigorous adherents of the Soviet
regime and its practices. For example, a leading member of the Soviet
academic folklore establishment, V. Chicherov, criticized Kriukova's neo-
epics as a likely product of the singer's collaboration with professional

"writers" simulating her style. As proof he cited the fact that when scholars who recorded traditional epics from her asked her to repeat the epic about the Cheliuskin expedition to the North Pole (which she allegedly composed and performed just a few months earlier), Kriukova was unable to reproduce "a single line," or the basic plot, or even the names of the heroes (Chicherov 1938: 128).

The moot question of the degree of authenticity can and should be clarified by folklorists while a few of those who worked in the Stalin era are still alive. I recently came across memoirs that offer credible, if anecdotal, evidence illuminating instances of the creation of "folk epics" (Zhovtis 1995). In some cases the singers were purely fictional. For instance, "*akyn* Maimbet", whose politically correct verse in Russian "translation" regularly adorned festive issues of Kazakhstan's leading newspapers in the mid-1930s and whose collected work was published, again in Russian, in 1934, was the creation of a certain Pavel Kuznetsov. This literary careerist found himself in trouble when the local Party officials decided to present the prolific *akyn* with a State reward; Kuznetsov saved his skin by claiming that "Maimbet" crossed the border into China with his family and cattle (such crossings did happen). Likewise, "The Ballad about Stalin," published in the famous collection, *Songs about Lenin and Stalin by Peoples of the USSR*, as a translation of the "Lapp epic" was apparently a creation of another literary hack catering to the official belief that every people of the USSR must have a folksong about Stalin.

The memoirs clarify some points about Dzhambul's authorship, even though the author notes that this problem is more complex than the incident in which he was involved could lead one to believe. In 1945 he, then a student at the university in Alma-Ata, was asked to re-translate Dzhambul's poem, "Dzhailiau" ("Highland Pasture") for an academic edition of Dzhambul's work because in the Kazakh original it had 40 lines—mostly landscape description with a remark that it was time to move to highland pastures; in the Russian translation by Konstantin Altaiskii the poem was expanded by some 30 lines. The difference consisted of an added panegyric to collective farming and Stalin's genius. Zhovtis' new translation, faithful to the original, was published, but in the last line the editor changed "our rich land" to "our happy land." In editions of Dzhambul's work of the post-Stalin era, the name of "the Genius of All Times and People" was simply deleted from all new printings, so that the reader of a pre-1958 edition of Dzhambul could get the impression that the great *akyn* sang Stalin's praises. Reading the same texts in post-1958 editions one could conclude that he never mentioned Stalin at all. Where the truth lies is for the present generation of folklorists to find out.

In conclusion, allow me to address to Dr. Zemtsovsky a couple of practical questions about the current state of folklore and ethnomusicology research in Russia: in what state is the so-called *Compilation of Russian Folklore* ("Svod russkogo fol'klora")? Is it still in progress or has it been abandoned? How far has it advanced? And what is your personal view on the merits of this project: do you see it as the vestige of the Soviet utopian gigantomania, or can it be truly useful, and in what ways?

The second question concerns the accessibility of folklore archives. In the Soviet era, the research of foreign scholars was hampered by zealous ideological bureaucrats whose task was to keep as much as possible out of reach. Today we hear stories from our colleagues about enterpreneurial, or perhaps simply financially desparate, archival administrators who are making awkward efforts to turn research needs into profit. For the privilege to work with research materials, unsuspecting visiting scholars are being charged exorbitant and arbitrary prices. Could you inform us about the situation in the folklore archives of Petersburg?

IZALY ZEMTSOVSKY

On Reading Three Responses

The three responses to our paper constitute three quite different viewpoints, a circumstance that attaches special interest to the discussion. Three scholars obviously present a broader picture of the subject, taking a position as if by concentric circles. Barbara Kirshenblatt-Gimblett gives a significant historical sketch of the last two-hundred years: she puts Russian experience into a European and worldwide context. Mark Slobin, although calling himself an outsider, knows the Russian language and Russian ethnomusicology, and he took part in two representative Soviet-American ethnomusicological dialogues as the chair and as a discussion leader. (By the way, Alma Kunanbaeva was a participant in the first dialogue in 1988, and I attended the second in 1989). Slobin's vision of the Soviet situation in folklore and folkloristics serves as an important addition to our view from within. In the aggregate of these two responses we receive a much more objective picture and more scholarly notion of traditional folklore and music in modern societies. We can see how much Soviet experience has in common with some others. All this is extremely useful.

Irina Gutkin, a native Russian and also an American scholar, emphasizes in her response the differentiation between Russian and Western societies. She is seeking "the inherent logic which informed that culture," and gives an essential supplement to Soviet folkloristics on the basis of modern Western literature. In her response, Irina Gutkin raises a few questions (actually six) to which I can give only laconic answers.

1. Why was converting the *mugam* "Baiaty-Shiraz" into "Baiaty-Moscow" deemed unacceptable, while numerous epics glorifying the Soviet state were greatly encouraged? This is because the Azerbaijani *mugam*, in contradistinction to the epic, represents a genre type with a "fixed" poetic text normally taken from traditional classic poetry. Therefore it was impossible to include new ideology in the *mugam*. The musicians attempted to disguise the same piece with a new title (as a playful gesture), but the *mugam* was banned nevertheless.

2. While composing new epics, singers used the same techniques in which they were skilled. This is correct. There were special official gatherings of folk singers where they "learned" to create so-called new folklore in a traditional way. They were told how to do that. We have to take into account the specific techniques of traditional oral composition with

their stable type of versification and their many *loci communes*. By the way, Yakut folk singers (*olonkhosuts*) can transform even a newspaper article into their very traditional style. There is one LP disc of Yakut music where it is impossible for an outsider who does not know the Yakut language to tell the difference between traditional epic or shaman singing and the song about Lenin.

3. To give "a thorough analysis as to exactly how and why the modern Siberian songs were falsified" would be really interesting and important, but it is impossible to do this in such a limited space. However, I have to admit that as a rule this was carried out by resorting to stylization. The falsifier worked like an amateur composer who creates a mixture of popular tunes by mixing so-called new folk songs with purely literary lines (i.e., in verse form, the routine couplet). The important criteria was that such works should be ideologically correct since nobody paid attention to the quality of the poetry at that time. Keen and quick-witted falsifiers were free to write as they pleased by regularly inserting the "correct" words and names. Such books were the best way to get promotion, awards, money, and notoriety.

4. In regards to GULAG folklore genres of "two very distinct cultures"—that of the criminals and that of the political prisoners— I can answer on the basis of the conference's material that this was so. There really were two distinct cultures, but there was no impassable wall between them and they were associated with each other. This conference gave the matter considerable thought.

5. Irina Gutkin would like to know my opinion concerning the "Compilation of Russian Folklore." First of all, we have had the idea to publish several such compilations in different Soviet republics. I could list a few such interesting undertakings, including Tajikistan and the folklore legacy of many Siberian and Far East peoples. As for me personally, I am not an admirer of this type of compilation. It seems that the idea of preparing such a series was noble enough but has been halted first of all because of lack of money. In principle, the series would be useful in summing up the bicentenary of Russian folkloristics from the contemporary standpoint of scholarly textology, and might be used to promote the popularization and education of a new generation.

6. Russian folklore archives are indeed a painful question. Commercialization of the archives has been taking place, so your information is correct. Allow me to give two examples, one from Moscow and the other from St. Petersburg. I remember one case when the Central Archives of the Arts asked for US $25,000 just for the right to copy the manuscript of one

piano transcription of an opera. In truth, this was a Jewish opera based on a Bible script, something criminal in itself. As a second example, the ethnomusicologists at the St. Petersburg Conservatory actually sell copies of their collection for considerable sums in the folklore market.

To sum up, let me say that our paper combines two genres—(1) an initial chronicle (and many concealed facts that we have brought to light for the first time) and (2) a kind of methodological warning: Be aware of two-faced communism in theory and in action. Be aware of its speculative and fatal method of playing and flirting with folklore and folk artists (as we now say, "ethnophores"). Be careful while using all Soviet facts and statements because the whole Soviet period was a time of all-consuming lies and fear. A few special and even outstanding exceptions only confirm the tragic rule. Understand that all actions and processes under the Soviet regime have touched on essence of national cultures under communism and that we therefore have to disentangle today all its after-effects.

Our article addresses all Western scholars with an appeal to revise their knowledge of our Soviet past in order to grasp the essence of our present. Our paper should most appropriately be the first part of a special indissoluble "disyllabic" article concerned with (1)Communism and Folklore and (2) Postcommunism and Folklore. We are still in the very beginning of both these undertakings. Who knows, maybe someday we will write a triptych with the third part as follows: (3) Postcommunism and "Postfolklore"! Everything is possible!

Finally I would like to thank the organizers of the conference and the initiators of this book, first of all Professor James Porter.

Part Two: Eastern Europe

ANKICA PETROVIĆ

The Status of Traditional Music in Eastern Europe

The investigation of traditional music in Eastern Europe is currently a means toward the better understanding, not only of music, but also of the general social and cultural situation there at a time of great political change. Similar cultural processes, and the uniform status of traditional music in Eastern Europe, suggest that first, we can conceive of that part of the Old World as a coherent geopolitical and cultural zone in spite of the fact that it comprises many different ethnic groups, and second, that the contemporary nation states of the region have been exposed to various historical and cultural currents.

Several factors have contributed to making East European culture generally unified, especially the traditional arts and traditional music. One is the predominantly Slavic origin of East European ethnic groups. Although the major East European geographic zones—the Carpathian Mountains, the Pannonian Plain, and the Balkan Peninsula—had long cultural traditions of their own, they were open to interaction with other cultural zones. This was the arena for the division of the Roman and Byzantine, and later of the Islamic religious spheres. Furthermore, most of Eastern Europe was for long periods under foreign rule: Austro-Hungarian in the northwest and Ottoman Turkish in the southeast. This meant, inevitably, that elements of the ruling cultures were incorporated, including music. Lastly, all the East European countries (except Greece) were exposed over the last fifty years to a forceful communist rule and ideology. Communism strictly directed and controlled the interpretation of all social, scientific, and cultural activities.

Today we are witnessing some intensive processes both of national sociopolitical consolidation and of the turbulent destruction of East European societies. There, cultural factors such as traditional music are used both as powerful tools for national recognition and as destructive forces in nationalistic manipulation.

This paper aims to focus critically upon the status of traditional music in Eastern Europe (excluding the countries that belonged to the former USSR) both from a historical perspective and in the contemporary period. It will try to present globally recognized forms and values of traditional music and the dominant theoretical approaches of the scholars and institutions that control the status of traditional music in this part of the world. Both approaches are treated as part of the discipline of ethnomusicology (known by various names at other times), which in Eastern Europe means, primarily, investigation of traditional or folkloric music. Eastern Europe has offered some very important theoretical and methodological directions and approaches in ethnomusicology; these can be recognized as having a specifically East European orientation.

The primary interests of East European scholars working in the field of traditional or folkloric music lay in native musical forms, which were in the main orally transmitted and secular in character. It is important to emphasize that the sources related to forms of traditional church music are commonly treated and presented as art music (except for the hymnal forms) and not as folk music. However, those who perform that music recognize their liturgical or paraliturgical musical forms as part of their folk tradition.

Some sporadic descriptions of and references to traditional music in Eastern Europe were compiled relatively early on, chiefly by foreign travelers, diplomats, or merchants. These observations offered information on musical context, instruments, and stylistic features, or they provided their own aesthetic experience of the singing, instrumental playing, or dancing of indigenous peoples.

The collecting and writing down of traditional songs were neglected until the nineteenth century. But the roots of some of these collections can be found in earlier periods. Peter Hektorović, a sixteenth century Croatian poet, was one of the first melographers of secular songs on Eastern Europe. He noted down two Croatian lyric songs (called *bugarštice*) that he heard from Dalmatian fishermen in 1557 and published them in the collection *Ribanje and ribarsko prigovaranje* (1568).[1]

The real interest in traditional music and other aspects of traditional culture in Eastern Europe developed in the period of romanticism among the educated elite. In the context of movements for national self-recognition, especially pan-Slavism, members of the elite felt that traditional music was a part of their precious cultural heritage. They also found that traditional music was a powerful means for provoking and strengthening national feelings. Newly-discovered forms of traditional music, and the values associated with them, had become the basis for cultural pride. In this climate, traditional music confronted Western musical achievements. Musicians, composers, folklorists, and musical amateurs became interested in collecting and noting down traditional music, primarily popular and urban folksongs. They wanted to popularize them mainly in a polished or arranged manner and to use their musical-thematic material as the basis for unexplored and "exotic" sounds in newer compositions. Rural folk music, especially from Balkanic areas, was generally unattractive or too difficult for proper understanding and notation by early ethnomusicologists and collectors.

Until recently, scholars in Eastern Europe focused predominantly upon the cultures within their own nation-states. They had little interest in the musical traditions and contemporary folk music of other nations. However, some melographers and folklorists became interested, in the nineteenth century, in the musical traditions of different Slavic peoples as the result of a shared pan-Slavic movement, as in the case of work by the Polish ethnographer Oskar Kolberg (1814–90), the Croatian music critic Franjo Ksaver Kuhač (1834–1911), and the Czech musicologist and painter Ludvik Kuba (1863–1956). Besides these, several figures are worth mentioning for their interest in East European traditional music: the Greek folklorist A.N. Sigalas, the Serbian composer Kornelije Stanković, the Hungarians István Bartálus, Béla Vikár, and others. Their basic merits can be seen in extensive published collections of folksongs and folklore. Some also offered preliminary but important theories on certain aspects of folk music style or the socio-cultural contexts in which they found folksongs in the second half of the nineteenth century. The melographers' interests, however, were not fully synchronized with the actual situation in the field of folk music. This was the early phase in the preservation of traditional music, but also the beginning of dynamic changes in the style and status of folk music that reflected newer processes in social and cultural life.

At the turn of the twentieth century, East European interest in folk music had intensified as demands for cultural self-recognition spread everywhere. Some common trends related to the treatment of cultural heritage, including folk music, and influenced other nations outside Europe. Thus, for instance, a marked similarity exists in the treatment of folk music between the Serbian melographer and composer Stevan Mokranjac (1856–1914) and the Armenian folklorist and composer Vartabed Komitas (1869–1935) even though they never established contact. Their common interests related to collecting numerous folksongs, establishing an authoritative ordering of religious chants in the Serbian and Armenian Orthodox liturgies, composing predominantly vocal music based on traditional native music patterns, and composing original masses in multi-part harmonic progression (drawing for this on traditional monodic chants). Moreover, there is an obvious similarity in their method of exploring folklore in their compositions. We cannot explain the similarities between Mokranjac's and Komitas's treatment of musical tradition as the result of accident, but rather as stemming from a centuries-long similarity in the socio-political and cultural history of their separate countries. These men had also common ideas on cultural identity and the role of music in expressing that identity.

A deeper understanding of, and presentation of, traditional music was limited until the present century with the appearance of the phonograph. The direct writing down on traditional music forms was restricting, not only for transcription but also for the process of analysis.

Radical changes in the treatment of folk music in East European countries arrived with the extensive scholarly activity of Zoltán Kodály (1888–1967) and Béla Bartók (1881–1945), who had begun systematic investigation of Hungarian folklore in 1905. These two prominent scholars, composers, educators, and artists developed methods and theories out of their new projects and on the basis of data related to their broad interests. Their primary aim was to "collect and study Hungarian peasant music" that was previously unknown, to observe folksongs as a living tradition, and to review the features of old, new, and mixed styles. Bartók also sought common patterns in the folk music of different nations: Slovaks, Hungarians, Croats, Serbs, Bulgarians, Turks, and Arabs and searched for the relationship between folk and art music. Their major interest in folk music emerged primarily from their activity as composers. Bartók understood that traditional and especially rural music offered new ideas for composition in terms of melody, rhythm, and formal structure. He began to apply rudimentary elements of Hungarian and Romanian folklore in his compositions at an early stage in his scholarly interest in traditional music, but his first such compositions were poorly received by the audiences in Budapest. This signifies that the application of authentic structural patterns which had emerged from Bartók's knowledge and experience of traditional music was still far removed from the norms and aesthetic experiences of the Hungarian cultural elite at the beginning of the twentieth century.

Kodály and Bartók evolved a new approach to folk music that began from the already established viewpoint of the Berlin school of comparative musicology. They also developed and coordinated new methods of collecting, analyzing, classifying and comparing folk music materials, thereby improving the recently founded discipline. Their common work on the scholarly and artistic promotion of folk music was received as extremely important for Hungarians but also for all ethnomusicologists in eastern Europe and indeed throughout the world, since some of their methods and approaches are still followed. Yet each of them had his own orientation and approach. While Bartók was interested in international comparative studies, searching to find common musical nuclei among traditions of several East European countries and to explain "ancestral cultural links between peoples who are today separated far from one another," Kodály's impetus was to establish the basis for an investigation of Hungarian cultural history.

Bartók's internationalism (ie., his interest in the musical traditions of countries surrounding his own) cannot be treated as a phenomenon *per se*. It can be explained, rather, as his real understanding of the complexity of East European socio-cultural processes as they are expressed through folk music. Bartók did not follow a hard nationalistic line, supporting theories about the absolute cultural autonomy of his own nation (as was common for that part of the world at the time). He "formed the hypothesis that a kinship or reciprocal influence existed between the folk music of linguistically differentiated peoples living within the borders of old Hungary" (Suchoff 1972: 557–571). Bartók's theoretical interest in the wide geographical dispersion of common musical patterns and elements was not, for him, relevant to the understanding of Hungarian traditional music exclusively, but rather for the insight he could achieve into general cultural processes. This is why he undertook fieldwork in Hungary, Slovakia, Romania, and Turkey, and worked hard to learn about traditional Bulgarian music and Milman Parry's collection of Serbo-Croatian folksongs. But theoretically and methodologically his comprehension of musical processes revolved around structural principles without comprehensive reference to the social setting. Nevertheless, although he avoided any discussion of social context, Bartók was accused "of a lack of patriotism" by the political authorities in 1920 because he had published an article on Romanian folk music.

Almost from the outset of their ethnomusicological activity, Bartók and Kodály collected folksongs in the field using the Edison phonograph. Bartók in particular was primarily responsible for developing fieldwork methods that included sound recordings. He then used these recordings for the transcription and analysis of sound data and was able to attain perfection in noting every small detail and fluctuation that his ear detected. Bartók's "exactness" in his highly descriptive transcriptions, which were published in numerous collections of East European traditional music, was often criticized for the reason that it was difficult to read.

My own conclusion is that Bartók, unlike most of his contemporaries and later ethnomusicologists, understood the morphological peculiarities of traditional music. It is my opinion that Bartók did not record such details in transcription just because of his excellent ear but also because he understood what each microtone, vibration, fluctuation, or rhythmical "flexibility" meant for the people in the culture and their musical style. His close connection with the field, where for decades he conducted his investigations annually, signals for us his deep understanding of the music. Bartók criticized the low transcription standards of some East European melographers and ethnomusicologists which he found a major obstacle in making structural analyses of East European traditional music. As a composer of western music and as one of the pioneers of ethnomusicology, he paid exclusive attention to analyzing the style of traditional music. The investigation of stylistic features and the status of traditional and folk music as it is understood in social terms was not yet familiar to Bartók and Kodály or most other European ethnomusicologists of their generation.

Over several decades of collaborative work, Bartók and Kodály established extensive folk music archives that, together with material collected later, became the main source for investigating Hungarian and other musical traditions. Giving priority in their research to the old rural traditions, they left behind an enormous opus, with published collections of folksongs from Hungary, Slovakia, Romania, Turkey, and Yugoslavia as well as studies on different theoretical and methodological aspects of this work. Their scholarly treatment of traditional music became a model in some East European countries, inspiring them to institute large archives of folk music or organize "systematic" investigation of native musical traditions (e.g., in the Baltic states and to some extent in Czechoslovakia and Yugoslavia). Over time, some of their theories and methods were criticized and replaced with new theories. Bartók's handling of the tradition in his compositions, too, was regarded as in some respects decadent in the early postwar communist period since it did not conform to the model of social-realist art in Eastern Europe.

In Romania the most notable treatment of traditional music was achieved by Constantin Brăiloiu (1893–1958), one of the most prominent ethnomusicologists of his generation. Acting in parallel with Bartók and Kodály and admiring their aims and accomplishments, Brăiloiu staked out original musicological and sociological approaches to music folklore. He treated oral tradition as a directed system that has to be defined primarily through analysis. With that goal in mind Brăiloiu developed fieldwork methods, applying the twin approaches of musicology and sociology, using recorded documents and transcriptions. To provide a systematic elaboration of the development of traditional music, Brăiloiu insisted on founding archives as strong, centralized institutions. Thus, he founded the Institutul de Folclor și Ethnografie in Bucharest (1928) and the International Folk Music Archives in Geneva (1944).

In addition to the usual scholarly means of presenting music traditions, Brăiloiu found recordings to be the most appropriate means of documentation and preservation. From 1930 to 1958 he edited and published, in Bucharest, Geneva, and Paris, 96 records of traditional music from Romania and different parts of the world. Finally, it is important to emphasize that Brăiloiu was one of the most active East European scholars in creating a new direction for ethnomusicology. He criticized previous theoretical treatments of European folk art and of non-European "primitive" music (for example, *Rezeptionstheorie* and what he termed "incoherent" theories of musical systems) and offered in his studies, some new directions for the field of *musical folklore* through sociological research. As one of the first European scholars to adopt the term *ethnomusicology* in 1954, Brăiloiu evinced interest in further radical change in the direction of the discipline.

Bartók, Kodály and Brăiloiu promoted the traditional music of Eastern Europe internationally through their collections and their original approaches to ethnomusicology and composition. They also contributed greatly to the recognition of the value of traditional music in the societies to which that music belonged. These three scholars are still acknowledged as the most prominent and productive ethnomusicologists in Eastern Europe.

The political changes in Eastern Europe after World War II brought immense changes in the status of the arts in general, and this affected the traditional arts especially. This period was largely reckoned to be very favorable for the official recognition of the folk arts, including traditional music. Folklore and ethnomusicology institutes, archives, or departments of folk music were established at universities. Musical folklore was systematically taught in the music high schools of Romania, Bulgaria, and Albania. Traditional music was recorded, classified, and discussed in the context of research projects and then presented at scholarly conferences and in many publications. The principal effort was aimed at finding appropriate systems of cataloging and classifying material in the field of traditional music and instruments. Musical terminology and the methods and principles of transcription were also the subject of intensive discussions that were organized either locally, or internationally within institutions in Eastern Europe. Some organizations in Poland, Czechoslovakia, Hungary, and Yugoslavia also collaborated with experts from Central Europe (Austria and Germany) in an effort to maintain previously established theoretical and methodological links within the discipline.

The socialist ideology that had been already developed and institutionalized in the USSR became the dominant model for the theoretical interpretation of traditional and folk music in most countries of Eastern

Europe. Gorky's definition of folklore as "the creativity of working class people" was adopted in most East Europe areas. Criticism of the previous decadent social classes by communist ideologues and privileging the working class or peasant class and their culture led to rigorous elimination of some forms and styles of traditional culture and to a preference for the cultural heritage of the working class. Following such ideology, traditional rural music together with new working-class and revolutionary folksongs—which were regarded as collective cultural creations—officially became the most favored subject for scholarly projects.

In some countries, cultural reality and actual scholarly interests were mutually incompatible. For example, the official orientation of folklorists and ethnomusicologists in the former Yugoslavia during the postwar period was directed toward investigating remnants of the rural traditional culture since the peasants were the most numerous category of the working class (ca. 75% of the total population until 1946). Immediately after 1946, a high percentage of the rural population was forcibly pushed into an urban environment in order to abandon their "primitive" conditions of life (i.e., their culture) and to accept new urban conditions from which they could become involved in the modernization and industrialization of their country. There they were unable to continue performing their traditional rural music since the function and social context of these forms were inappropriate to the new urban society in which the newcomers found themselves. Further, although ethnomusicologists were very active in recording and archiving the "precious remains" of traditional rural music, rural songs or dances could be heard on radio programs, or on the stage only in stylized and elaborate forms, until the 1970s.

The official presentation of traditional music on the stage was confined, in Eastern Europe, to amateur groups of singers, players, and dancers. Their activities were, of course, organized and supervised by the government. The late 1960s brought to Eastern Europe the "festivalization" of traditional music, a phenomenon that also involved the presentation of newer folk music styles: for example, Greek *rebetika* songs [2] and Yugoslav "newly composed folk music." Very popular from the 1970s, this trend in Yugoslavia was poorly received by the experts because it broke the principle rule of folk creativity, namely collective creation. The composers and poets of these new "folksongs" were known, but their music was officially anathema since it did not follow the rules of traditional folk creativity. For this reason they had to avoid the controls of official cultural policy and followed instead the taste of consumers of their music and market influences, implementing this direction at many festivals and in the mass media.

In the last two decades, traditional music was also a source of inspiration for pop and rock music groups in Eastern Europe. The music of these groups was enormously popular and promoted traditional culture among the younger generation. Even so, these trends did not get appropriate recognition from the scholars and from the leaders of cultural policy. Meanwhile, the Hungarians and Bulgarians developed an interest in the revival of their ancestral music. Some younger scholars attempted to define anew the essence of their nation's traditional music as it had been found in the field and to present it on stage in an authentic but "elite" mode of interpretation.

From the early 1950s the majority of ethnomusicological projects undertaken in East European institutions had an anthological or monographic character and related mainly to research into local and regional musical traditions. Very often the borders of the scholars' interests had to be restricted along contemporary administrative lines that did not correspond to the real dispersal of some traditional forms of music and their attendant phenomena. In most cases, therefore, research was limited to one's own regional and narrow national interests. Such studies contradicted the general socialist proclamation on social and cultural internationalism. Monographic studies of this kind, however, very often neglected existing cultural links and the relevant socio-cultural processes. In short, to avoid proclaiming meaningless socialist dogma, scholars were often constrained to ignore some connections that actually existed between and among cultures. The pressure of ideology thus had an unavoidably distorting influence on research.

Some attempts at comparative investigation into traditional music in Eastern Europe emerged and aimed at discovering the basis morphological principles in folk music of different ethnicities; these were usually realized within Slavic peoples (e.g., the works of Rubtsov, Czekanowska, Goshovski, Zemtsovsky) or within Finno-Ugric groups (Vikár, Szöke). However, existing cultural connections, as they had been expressed through traditional forms of music within heterogeneous ethnicities (for example within Balkan nations) were greatly neglected since they did not correspond to the official interpretation of cultural history.

Studies of musical traditions outside national boundaries or outside Slavic cultures were not accepted or supported in East European countries. Polish scholars and institutions alone carried out projects of this kind (e.g., in Central Asia). Research into minority musical traditions was undertaken mainly in cases when music of one's own nation was performed outside one's country by an expatriate minority. Recent exceptions to such an exclusive view have led, in some centers, to a certain internationalization of research interest, especially among scholars of the younger generation.

East European scholars also began to take a greater interest in more recent theories of traditional music as they were introduced from Western sources. Some theories, especially those derived from linguistics or anthropology, stood little chance of official recognition in this part of the world. In fact, only a small number of experts had communication with the Western world, that is, were informed about *other* trends and theoretical concepts in ethnomusicology. No "serious" scholars were willing to deal with popular culture. It was unusual to quote or apply the theories or relevant findings of contemporary Western scholars, with the exception of Poland. Senior scholars were ready, even in the late 1980s, to term contemporary Western approaches as "decadent" or "bourgeois ethnomusicology" in order to protect their own doctrine.

Such accusations deterred East European scholars from studying musical traditions and their transformations objectively. We were obliged to remain deaf for decades to many socio-cultural phenomena as they were reflected through music. In many cases we were not supposed to find the real roots of traditional sounds or to discover the entire spectrum of cultural influences. We had to favor certain traditions, to neglect or totally deny others, and to overlook the roots of smoldering nationalism. Often we were not supposed to trace the transformation of music (i.e., of society) for fear that we might discover some "displeasing" sounds — that is, displeasing aspects of society. That is why ethnomusicologists from Eastern Europe were supervised and investigated by the secret police if we did something that contravened official doctrines and trends.

In offering this critical review of the status of traditional music in Eastern Europe in a period of major social and cultural change, I do not think that, after the collapse of the communist system, the coming period will bring radical metamorphosis in the treatment of tradition in music in that part of the world. Some traditions may be recognized again or become over-revived, like Serbian epics during the latest nationalistic hysteria. Unfortunately the new nationalist politics, when extended into the most cruel confrontations in the former Yugoslavia, lead to human and cultural extermination. Traditional music once more becomes a powerful tool for the manipulation of the masses and a weapon in ethnic strife. It is now a moral question whether we should permit our traditions, our knowledge, and our discipline to serve extremist political systems rather than scholarship.

Traditional music by its very innocence tempts tyrants to use and distort it for political purposes. There is much work that young scholars can accomplish today in revealing and unmasking such abuse and in searching to find new values in East European traditions. Through such attention, both our discipline and traditional music itself will benefit.

Notes

1. *Bugarštica* is a kind of Croatian narrative song from the period between the fifteenth and eighteenth centuries.
2. *Rebetika* are Greek urban songs from the beginning of this century that were rediscovered and popularized in the 1970s by the younger generation.

CAROL SILVERMAN

Comments on the Study and Practice of Ethnomusicology in Eastern Europe

I would like to begin my comments with a tribute to Ankica Petrović, conceived with the ideas of Valery Tishkov, Director of the Institute of Ethnology and Anthropology of the Russian Academy of Sciences and Minister for Nationalities for the Russian government. In an article entitled "The Crisis in Soviet Ethnography," Tishkov writes that "The body of our science is sick with several ailments at once. The most serious and least perceptible of these is the absence of introspection and self-analysis" (1992:377). Filling in this absence is precisely what Ankica Petrović has done both in this article and in her other work (1994). She explores the relationship between the writing of ethnomusicology and the social, economic and historical conditions which informed those writings. Yet the argument is not as simple as ethnomusicology being a product of social and political conditions. Rather, ethnomusicology has also shaped these political and social conditions. Thus in the period of Romantic nationalism, collectors were not merely at the beck and call of philosophy and nationalism; rather, music collecting generated philosophy and nationalism. For example, the writings of Balkan music collectors such as Vuk Karadžić can be considered simultaneously musical collections and political philosophy (Lockwood 1971).

If we examine the works of Ankica Petrović, we will see several other prophetic intellectual strands which recall Tishkov's recent formulations of how to ameliorate the crisis in post-socialist scholarship. Tishkov claims that Soviet ethnography, with its reified vocabulary of various levels of ethnicity and its simplistic insistence on the naturalness of ethnic groupings, failed to explore how ethnicity actually worked in everyday life. He asked, "how do citizens of Moscow experience their Jewishness, Armenianness or Russianness?" (1992:375). Petrović has written precisely on this issue, focusing on music. For example, in her analysis of Serbian, Croatian, Muslim, and Jewish music in Bosnia, she showed how one tune could be shared by all four groups but interpreted differently in style, meter, language or dialect, text and meaning (1988; 1990b). She further analyzed the multiple forms of Islamic influence, eschewing the simplistic party-line obligatory rejection of non-Slavic elements which many other Balkan researchers espoused (1988). She also researched the question of gender in musical performance, a topic extremely rare in socialist accounts of folk arts (1990a).

    Tishkov wrote that Soviet ethnography failed to pay attention to urban contexts, precisely those places where ethnicity is played out at close range (1992:375). Petrović, however, focused on the city of Sarajevo and its musical relationships in various contexts. Tishkov claimed that Soviet ethnography failed to encourage or even allow long-term fieldwork (1992:374), something to which Petrović committed herself. And finally, Tishkov speaks of the Soviet failure to address ethical problems in field-work, such as moral obligations to one's informants and implications of research for national policy (1992:375–6). This is a topic on which Petrović is currently working, specifically the use of music during war in terms of nationalist rhetoric and imagery (1994).

    One can certainly argue that the Soviet Union was more repressive than Yugoslavia, and thus Petrović's innovative contributions were more possible in Yugoslavia than in the USSR. Yet even in Yugoslavia, ideological agendas were strictly set in every institute and university, and deviants were investigated and persecuted. An example from socialist Bulgaria may illustrate the enforced lack of communication between scholarly institutes. Since there was a separate Institute of Music, a separate Institute of Folklore and a separate Institute of Ethnography, labor was divided: the ethnomusicologist would notate the melody of a song, the folklorist would write down the text and the ethnographer would document the ritual in which it was sung. This might have been great teamwork had they talked to each other; unfortunately they did not.

    I would like to expand on a few of Petrović's points by enlarging her premise which I may restate as follows: Just as ethnomusicology as a discipline is not merely a by-product of politics, so music itself is not merely derivative of politics—it is constitutive of politics. Music, then is not a reflection of politics—it is political. Music shapes politics and economics and social life as well as being shaped by them. As I have often said to political scientists: If music were, indeed mere entertainment, why, then, was folk music censored in Iran, why did the Bulgarian socialist government prohibit the instrument *zurna* and the musical form *kjucék*, why was epic poetry censored in Central Asia and why was Western rock music severely regulated in every socialist nation (Silverman 1996).

    I would like to emphasize the point that music mobilizes—both for official purposes (socialist, democratic, or nationalist) and for subversive purposes (socialist, democratic, or nationalist). Numerous histories can be cited, for example the use of music in Breton and Catalonian regional movements, in Nazi culture, and in all American wars. Thus, I disagree with Ankica Petrović about "the very innocence" of folk music. On the other hand, I agree with her observation that folk music is continually used for political purposes. Examples of this phenomenon from socialist Eastern Europe are easy to list, especially in terms of centralized government sponsorship: in Bulgaria, the government poured huge amounts of money into the amateur folk music movement through village music collectives and through festivals. Festivals promoted a mono-ethnic image of the state and fostered a static view of the peasant past (Silverman 1983, 1989). The government also sponsored professional ensembles and folk music schools, both of which promoted a unified national style which displayed the modernization of the nation's folklore through elaborate choral and instrumental arrangements and staged choreography (Buchanan 1995). In both spheres, festivals and ensembles, minority ethnicities were censored and repressed. Official musical policy created in Bulgaria an official discourse of legitimation—that is, folklore in the service of building the socialist nation. I might venture to point out that socialist nation-building was somewhat similar to the nation-building of the Romantic nationalist period of the nineteenth century, where the soul of the nation was supposedly embedded in its folklore. And the current use of folk music to mobilize for nationalist agendas is yet the latest chapter in the political uses of Balkan folklore. Both among nationalist Croatians and nationalist Serbs there is a huge repertoire of war songs, many of which are rewritten folk songs from the socialist era (Petrović 1994).

If these examples suffice to illustrate the official government-sponsored side, let us turn to the subversive side, i.e., how music is a force for resistance. We are well indebted to the British school of Cultural Studies for first pointing out that popular culture can sometimes serve as an agent of hegemony but can also be a form of resistance to hegemony (Hall and Jefferson 1976). Indeed, Sabrina Ramet has recently pointed out that rock music was the music of the revolutions of 1989 (1994). Rock groups in Eastern Europe not only made political statements in the texts of their songs, but the musical form of rock itself was anti-government because of its association with the West. Ramet further claims that the censorship of rock music made it even more popular (1994:8). I believe her argument could be extended to certain forms of folk music. In the case of Bulgaria, for example, censored Muslim musical forms and texts continued to existed in more private covert realms, such as the family. More striking, however, was the emergence of the genre of wedding music as a countercultural mass youth movement, complete with superstars and inflated prices. Wedding music, with its loudness, electric amplification, Western instruments, daring speed and technique, rock and jazz influences, and eclectic musical borrowings from film, classical and pop epitomized youth culture even more than rock music in Bulgaria. The fact that it was associated with Roma (Gypsies) and Turks who did not officially exist in the socialist Bulgaria of the 1980s made it doubly subversive.

This leads to my final point that we need to reject the dichotomy socialist/post-socialist as too simplistic. Many of the musical phenomena and changes discussed in this conference began significantly earlier than 1989 in Eastern Europe and earlier than 1991 in the Soviet Union. As the interplay of unofficial and official music shows, the socialist period was not a stagnant era, rather it was extremely dynamic. Further, musical changes were not merely products of pro- or anti-government ideology. Musical changes had much to do with processes such as youth alienation, urbanization, economics (black-market or legitimate), and the role of intellectuals. For example, wedding music in Bulgaria was not only anti-government— it was also a viable niche in the second economy, especially for Roma. In addition, it was a youth movement that successfully bridged urban and rural contexts (Silverman 1996). It is thus important to analyze the various roles a certain musical style or instrument plays, not just its political role. And within the realm of politics, it is important to ask which musical genres become countercultural at a particular historical moment and why? And what is the political relationship between music and other expressive arts such as dance and costume? And finally, what makes some musics counter-cultural—is it the style, the text, or the instrumentation?

It is perhaps easy to see how music mobilizes thought and actions in a centralized socialist setting where there is an easily identified official ideology plus an oppositional covert counterculture. Indeed, we should be reminded of Bernice Martin's observation that all culture simultaneously reinforces the existing order and offers alternative visions (1979:87). This dialectic on hegemony applies to in capitalist/democratic societies as well as socialist societies. We should also be reminded that socialists do not have a monopoly on repression. To take an example of the making of official ideology in a supposedly democratic Balkan society, let us examine Greece. In Greece, the furor over erasing and replacing word Macedonia in song or print is a daily phenomenon. Michael Herzfeld argues convincingly that Greek folkloristics developed to glorify the supposedly unbroken cultural line from classical to modern Greece and to specifically deny Ottoman influence in Greek folklore (1982).

Closer to home, here in the United States one may observe the making and critiquing of official discourse about folk art. The National Endowment for the Arts, for example, has adopted a set of criteria for folk arts which is echoed on the state and city level by many agencies. Some scholars have found these criteria rigid, exclusionary, and arbitrary, in part because they privilege membership by birth and a naturalistic concept of local community (Shuman 1993; Kirshenblatt-Gimblett 1988). Similarly, a lively debate about the usefulness of the term "authenticity" and the concept of "cultural conservation" is currently active among folklorists (Feintuch 1988, Hufford 1994). In the United States one can also find forms of expressive culture that move from counterculture to official. Rap and break dancing, for example, were street based forms of counterculture which became mainstream as they entered Hollywood and big business, yet they still exist on the streets, and can also be found at folk festivals. We see, then, that ideology, both official and unofficial, and its expression in folk arts are players in a highly charged interchange about hegemony.

In conclusion, Ankica Petrović's article urges us to consider seriously the political and social milieu of the writing of ethnomusicology. I hold that the analysis of socialist and post-socialist societies can provide us with insights into our own folklore, for it highlights the political dimension of culture, a project which involves competing rights to define, to fund, to regulate, and to contest.

TIMOTHY RICE

Bulgarian Folkloristics and Ethnomusicology at and after the Fall of Communism

On November 10, 1989, a number of prominent government officials from within the Communist Party deposed Todor Zhivkov as party chairman. Arrested and later put on trial, Zhivkov had ruled for twenty-five years, longer than any of his contemporaries in the Soviet Union and Eastern Europe. These "events," as they were called, led to a long and difficult transition, which continues to the present, from totalitarianism to multiparty democracy.

Inspired by Ankica Petrović's thoughtful and touching paper, this response describes and interprets the role and work of Bulgarian folklorists in the periods immediately before and after these events. It explores three of her most important points as they apply to the Bulgarian case: first, the way in which "communism strictly directed and controlled the interpretation of all social, scientific, and cultural activities"; second, the pre- and post-communist attitudes toward popular and urban culture; and third, whether and to what extent folkloristics and music scholarship have changed in the post-communist era. In offering the following interpretation, which might be read by some as a critique, I am deeply aware of the sticky webs of culture and politics within which my Bulgarian colleagues operated from 1944 to 1989. Those of us from abroad who worked in the Soviet Union and Eastern Europe during the communist period experienced some of communism's capacity for terror in very personal ways, but our empathy and understanding were limited because, unlike our colleagues from those countries, we could always leave.

Folkloristics in the Last Years of Communism

Totalitarianism tries, and in important ways succeeds, to assume total control of every domain of life, starting with the political and the economic but including the cultural or, in its terms, the ideological. No one in Bulgaria could escape these totalizing strategies and practices and their brutalizing effects, least of all folklorists, who were called upon under the communists to use their folkloristics to define the Party's nationalist vision in suitably respectable, scholarly terms. Contributing to the linkage between the folk, the national, and the political during the communist period was the word narodna (feminine form). The phrase narodna muzika is appropriately glossed as "folk music," and refers to both musical practices in rural areas and more contemporary practices with supposed roots in rural tradition. In the country's pre-1989 name, *Narodna Republika Bûlgaria* (People's Republic of Bulgaria), *narodna* is properly glossed as "people's," and refers to the Party's rule in the name of the people, the dictatorship of the proletariat. *Narodna kultura* usually refers to "national culture," and *narodna* is the first definition given to the English word "national" in my English-Bulgarian dictionary. Thus, while the English language helps us separate conceptually (even when they should perhaps be linked) the government's politics, the nation's culture, and the oral traditions and lore of the ostensibly simple, perhaps rural, folk, the Bulgarian language, in the word *narodna*, conflates all these categories into a densely woven fabric that envelops everyone's feelings and thoughts and makes the study, practice, and appreciation of folklore impossible to disentangle from the threads of politics and nationalism.[1]

This enmeshment of politics and folkloristics can be demonstrated in the myriad activities, in addition to field collecting and the writing of scholarly articles and books, in which folklorists engaged during the communist period. The director of the Folklore Institute of the Bulgarian Academy of Sciences (BAN), Todor Ivanov Zhivkov (no relation to the party chairman), served on the Party's Central Committee. Folklorists wrote innumerable journalistic articles, interpreting and prescribing the proper attitude toward *narodna* practices to ordinary people, who read newspapers voraciously. They wrote record-jacket notes for the state-run recording company. They participated in, guided, and commented upon the *obrabotvane* ("arranging," "improving") of traditional, rural practices for presentation in concerts and festivals and on radio and television. Many of them—including Nikolaj Kaufman, the most prolific collector of folksongs during the communist period—created such arrangements, and the musical folklorist Mihail Bukureshtliev became at one point the director of the "State Ensemble of Folk Songs and Dances" founded by the composer Filip Kutev. Folklorists organized and sat on the juries of countless amateur and professional music and folklore festivals, each designed to control the proper presentation of "national culture" (*narodna kultura*), particularly in its "folk" (*narodni*, pl.) forms, to "the people" (*narod*).

It is probably fair to say that folklorists' careers in the Soviet Union and Eastern Europe included a better balance between academic reflection and practical action than those of most American folklorists and ethnomusicologists, a balance consonant with Marxist philosophy. Certain scholars dutifully weighed in with interpretations of the relevance of folklore, particularly in its modernized forms, for the formation of contemporary, national culture. On the other hand, some folklorists tended to bracket the political implications of their work, and they did so in at least three ways. First, their practical activities could be justified economically, for they received honoraria for every article, arrangement, or jury served on, money that supplemented significantly their meager salaries for positions in various institutes of BAN or at universities and conservatories. Their organizing or directing work could even turn into a second job, for example as artistic director of a performing ensemble. Second, they spent a great deal of time in the field, collecting material from the oldest generation of performers, those raised before communism, whose lore they interpreted in largely formalistic terms or in connection to a past, pre-communist life rather than to the present. Third, they adopted the English the word "folklore" (*folklor*) to describe their scholarly discipline and its object of study, replacing the older concept of *narodno umotvorenie* (folk creation). This renaming conveniently erases the political implications, especially problematic in the communist period, of a discipline or subject matter with the word *narodno* in it.

The crosscurrents that must have vexed Bulgarian folklorists are well illustrated by their response to so-called "wedding music" (*svatbarska muzika*), the most dynamic and politically charged form of music during the last decade of the communist period. The genre's name labels the context, but more tellingly distinguishes it from *narodna muzika*, which was managed and controlled by the state. Wedding music, although it used many of the same forms and styles typical of *narodna muzika*, flourished outside state control in the hands of Gypsy musicians who became rich playing for weddings financed by private wealth that had been accumulated through petty trading, farming, craftsmanship, and the selling of personal services. Whereas state-controlled *narodna muzika* produced—an apt verb—by professional and amateur *narodni ansembli* and *narodni muzikanti* and recorded for state-run media had congealed into a unchanging symbol of the state, wedding music during the 1980s exploded in importance as a popular form played by innovative musicians eager to outdo each other in fiery virtuosity and improvisation; the most famous of these was the clarinetist Ivo Papazov. As open dissatisfaction with communism grew with *glasnost*, *perestroika*, and a crisis over the repression of Muslim minorities, the freedom of expression in wedding music became a metaphor for political freedom.

Bulgarian folklorists' responses to wedding music ranged from negative to positive, but all were conditioned by their understanding of *narodna muzika*. The negative responses were of two kinds. Some found wedding music, with its purposefully raucous, undisciplined sound, "cheap" and "tasteless kitsch." They claimed the guiding principle was an inartistic appeal to popular taste in contrast to the consciously artistic modes of presentation of "arranged folklore" and the high artistic standards claimed for older, "authentic" forms "from the wellspring" that, they claimed, had been molded by and were true expressions of the genius of the Bulgarian people. A second group of folklorists recognized the potentially subversive character of musical freedom and condemned what they called the "aggressive" sound of the music, employing the same adjective used to condemn Muslim cultural practices such as speaking Turkish or wearing *shalvari* (Muslim women's baggy trousers). The positive responses were also of two kinds. Some recognized in wedding music the dynamic principles of variation and improvisation in oral tradition that were inherent in many definitions of folklore. It occurred to some scholars that what was called folklore in Bulgaria had become calcified and classicized products for production and consumption, whereas wedding music involved processes that were being worked out by the people according to their tastes and were functioning according to their needs. These scholars pointed out the fit between wedding music and their own criteria for what constituted folklore. A second positive interpretation involved the claim that wedding music was not a radically new kind of music as its innovative character may have suggested to some people. Rather, it had its roots in Bulgarian traditions of the *chalgadzhii*, a Bulgarian variant of a Turkish word meaning "musicians" and referring to nineteenth-century professional town musicians, many of whom were Gypsies. Wedding musicians in the 1980s, this view claimed, were nothing more than latter-day reincarnations of nineteenth-century *chalgadzhii*, whom Bulgarian scholars had ignored in recent years in their search for the "wellsprings" of village music.[2]

These responses, whether positive or negative, indicate the extent to which any form of cultural production, in this case musical production, had political implications for folklorists during the communist period. Even the positive responses could be interpreted politically—though I can't comment on the intent of those who held these views—as an attempt to assimilate wedding music into the category of *narodna muzika* and into the honorable history of Bulgarian tradition. If the assimilation were successful, it would have the effect of minimizing both the freshness of wedding music and the differences between it and *narodna muzika*. An interpretive merging of the two genres would also diminish wedding music's potential for carrying anti-communist political meaning and eliminate its symbolic capacity for referencing the condition of repressed Muslim minorities.

It would be difficult to argue that the musical freedom inherent in wedding music caused the fall of communism, but it certainly was one of many manifestations of discontent with communism. It was a domain where people could begin to experience the power they had in a totalitarian society. Its cultural vitality also forced folklorists, whether sympathetic or unsympathetic, to deal in one way or another with a popular genre that erased their artificially created boundaries between urban and rural forms of expression.

Folkloristics after the Fall

To assess the direction of Bulgarian folkloristics after the fall of communism in 1989, I consulted the pages of Bulgaria's main folklore journal, *Bûlgarski Folklor*, published during the first four years of the post-communist period, 1990 to 1993. Evident in that journal are both continuity and change. The continuities include an undiminished interest in rural traditional practices and in the relation between whatever is defined as folklore and contemporary life. The differences include a new critical perspective unfettered by a single ideology and an engagement with once forbidden themes and practices.

The first two issues from the post-communist period, 1990 (1,2), contain articles with a predictable emphasis on descriptions of rural practices. This is hardly surprising since they probably had gone to press before "the events" of November 10, 1989. Typical articles include "The Wedding Night in Slavic Wedding Rites" (1990/1), "Problems from the Field Study of Proverbs and Sayings" (1990/2), and "Images of Vines and Grapes in Bulgarian Practical Folk Art" (that is, bread and embroidery designs) (1990/2). Another article, "Folk music at the Bulgarian Radio (1971–1988)" (1990/2), is a good example of folklorists' willingness to interpret the contemporary life of folklore. Published after the Fall, it could have been a critical examination of the political function of radio broadcasting during the communist period. Undoubtedly written before the Fall, it is a classic example of one group of state employees, the folklorists, praising another group, the radio programmers. The author's sunny conclusion: "The radio displays the richest and most beneficial laboratory for studying, researching, analyzing, and predicting the processes of folk performing art among us" (p. 83).[3]

The third issue of 1990 is the first one to reflect the changes of 1989, a rather fast response for academics. Dimitrina Kaufman's "From the Chalgija of the National-Revival Period to Contemporary Wedding Orchestras" makes a case for the historical continuity of contemporary wedding orchestras with the small bands and ensembles of "city culture" in Bulgaria from the late nineteenth to mid-twentieth century. The elite, who came to control Bulgarian culture in the communist period, dismissed this "city culture" as remnants of "bourgeois culture," and so it was suppressed for the most part. Kaufman points out that, at the beginning of the century, city songs and tunes were more prestigious than the village ones promoted by the communists. What makes the article post-communist in its outlook is her admission that urban culture included all ethnic groups, and that Gypsies provided a common element in urban culture. She writes of an absence of chauvinism and racism and a free exchange of musical ideas between Serbian, Bulgarian, and Romanian musicians in northwestern Bulgaria where these traditions mix. All these points serve as an important corrective to some of the main nationalist distortions of tradition under the communists, distortions in which folklorists had to participate.

In the same issue Georg Kraev, in his "Mythology of Urban Folk Holidays, or Toward a Mythology of the Contemporary," is the first to mention explicitly November 10, 1989. He cannot bring himself to name the ideology of the preceding period, preferring to label it the period of the "totalitarian nation." The totalitarian government incorrectly conflated the village with the folk or the national, and he claims that within a mere 120 days after the "events," urban folklore has changed from a negative to a positive connotation and is now a legitimate object of study. To refer to village culture, he replaces the old phrase, *izvoren folklor* ("folklore from the wellspring"), with the phrase, "classical folklore," and asks: what are contemporary folk holidays and how are they celebrated? His answer is that in the "totalitarian nation" so-called folk holidays were actually based on city folklore. "In these conditions the Bulgarian village had practically nothing in common with its classical predecessor—the village community of the middle ages." Bulgarian villagers in the communist period lived in an urban style and celebrated the socialist urban holidays. "The unofficial culture of the totalitarian nation is urban folklorism (*folklornost*)." Though he admits that a conflation of the village with the national was a tendency since the national-revival period of the mid-nineteenth century, the totalitarian nation took it to the absolute extreme. "The idea of Bulgarian folklore became the image of political kitsch."

The politics of Nikolaj Kaufman's "The Jewish Songs of My

Mother" in the same issue are more subtle. He had written articles on Jewish music before 1989, but had also failed to mention the obvious Jewish character of a number of melodies in his collection of Bulgarian city songs, *Bûlgarski gradski pesni* (Sofia: Bulgarian Academy of Sciences, 1968). The communists' overweening ethnic nationalism had surely made him leery of advancing such claims about an ostensibly Bulgarian tradition. He must have felt free of that nationalism and comfortable proclaiming his own ethnicity when he published these highly personal songs with Yiddish texts written in the Cyrillic alphabet.

The fourth and final issue of 1990 contains a thoughtful, painful, exculpatory article by Todor Ivanov Zhivkov, head of the Folklore Institute. Entitled "Folklore—a Care and Concern of Society," he revisits a theme he treated frequently during the communist period. He seems to mount a defense of the old approach to folklore in the communist period—and the pre-communist period, written as it was on the occasion of the 100th anniversary of Ivan Shishmanov's seminal article, "The Meaning and the Purpose of our Ethnography." Reflecting new sensibilities, he writes of the communist period as "after World War II" rather than "after the 9th of September," the date set for the communist takeover and the most frequently used code phrase for the communist period at that time. He points out that many folklorists like Raina Katsarova, Elena Stoin, and Hristo Vakarelski fought attempts to ideologize every folklore manifestation, but then admits, "We who devoted ourselves to the study, preservation, and sanctioning of folklore [in the communist period] stand today here with our achievements, our wounds, and our sins" (p. 59). Admitting that "folklore is an especially fruitful field for ideological modeling" (p. 60), he is clearly ambivalent about folklorists' role in that modeling. Folk ensembles and choirs started out, he claims, as a fruitful development but then became "a mere cultural facade." On the other hand, he worries that "To deny the accomplishments of the radio and television, of Balkanton [the national recording company], of our presses means to hurry to throw out the useful and necessary of our culture" (p. 61). Finally, he ends with a manifesto that Bulgarian folklorists in the future will study all new forms, youth culture, and ethnic groups, perhaps hoping that these activities will wash away the "sins" of the past.

These progressive articles, to turn one of the communists' favorite phrases ironically on its head, exist alongside the continuing publication of articles about "classical folklore" topics, and the first two issues of 1991 have no articles reflecting the explicit or implicit manifestos of the last half of 1990. However, the third issue of 1990 is devoted completely to the newly sanctioned topic of urban folklore. The issue, titled "The Town and Folklore," provides an instant corrective to decades of neglect. Some of the articles in the issue, with titles like "Printed Jokes from Gabrovo: On the Origins of the Image of a Bulgarian Industrial Town" and "Town and Joke," seem cautiously retrospective and historical, ways to avoid the inherent dangers of relevance learned in a totalitarian state. More interesting are those that provide the first detailed descriptions of the political events after November 10, 1989, interpreted by folklorists as contexts for folkloric display and the working out of folkloric processes: Iveta Todorova-Pirgova, "Event and Ritual: The Student Strikes as Catalyst of a Cultural Synthesis"; Radost Ivanova, "'Goodbye Dinosaurs, Welcome Crocodiles': Political Meetings and Their Slogans Studied from a Folklorist's Point of View"; and Anatol Anchev, "Political Folklore after November 10, 1989." The best joke in this collection, by the way, tells of Vladko Zhivkov, Todor Zhivkov's son, coming home obviously concerned about the recent political events. As he enters the house, he shouts "Oh God, God!" Hearing him, Todor Zhivkov answers, "Stop that! Since they deposed me, you can just call me 'Dad'!"

Perhaps the most important article in this vein details the most striking bit of political theater in the aftermath of "the events": during the summer of 1990 students went on strike and formed a semi-permanent gathering of protesters, called the "Town of Truth," in a park near the home of then-president Petûr Mladenov. Magdalena Elchinova and Valentina Rajcheva, in their "On the Characteristics of a New Type of Cultural Phenomenon (The written texts with drawings created during the students' occupational strike and 'The Town of Truth')," study the use of parody and the structure and function of the artistic forms used during the strike and demonstration. Led by youths pushing for faster progress toward democratization, the Town of Truth featured permanent residents who lived in homes/tents, cultivated yards, or spaces between tents, and created "living complexes" (the Bulgarian name for urban neighborhoods of high-rise apartment buildings) grouped by political party. The "streets" each had their own names: "Without Communism Street," "Toward Communism Street," which was "closed because of repairs" (one of the most frequently seen signs around Sofia during the communist period) and "Path to America Boulevard." The "Town of Truth" had a city square dedicated as "an arena for public disputes," a bookstore, a medical station, a church, a press center, and a mayor, who changed every day. In many ways their account mirrors the detailed ethnography previously reserved for "folkloric customs," though they conclude by claiming that the approaches relevant to the study of the "texts" produced in this town are different from the approaches used in the study of so-called "classical folklore texts."

One other article in this issue deserves to be singled out for attention: Milena Benovska-Subkova's "UFOs, Poltergeist, Mysticism, and Spiritual Crisis: Contemporary Myth-Creation and Folk Tradition." This article responds to a deep interest in and curiosity about paranormal, spiritual, and mystical phenomena during the communist period among Sofia intellectuals, a need largely unmet by their own press and satisfied by cadging books from foreign visitors. The article taps into an important, but previously undiscussable, feature of the Bulgarian intellectual landscape, a theme taken up again in the 1993/5 special issue devoted to "The Paranormal," with articles on seances, dreams, astrology, extrasensory perception, and alternative medicine.

Over the next two years (1991/4, 1992, and 1993) new themes largely avoided or suppressed during the totalitarian period continue to emerge, with a similar balance between rather traditional, even backward-looking accounts and more up-to-date articles with contemporary political implications. Among the former, Todor Dzhidzhev's "Features of the Stylistic Envelope of Many Contemporary Instrumental Groups of Bulgarian Folk Music" (1991/4) is a potentially interesting topic, but he was a jury member in the festivals that tried to control the playing style and repertoire of wedding bands in the totalitarian period, and he continues to worry about issues of poor taste, a passé and compromised rhetorical stance in the 1990s.

In 1992/1 two reports on folk festivals, standard fodder for journal and newspaper articles during the communist period, document folklorists' changed activities and changes in the festivals themselves in the post-communist period. Nikolaj Kaufman, in "Koprivshtitsa '91," reports on the success of the national folk festival that occurred in "these difficult days" in spite of the fact that many cultural workers had been laid off. Although he feared "anarchy," everything went off well; he claimed that some of the 17,000 participants came on foot, an excellent example of folklorists creating folklore. There was the usual commission of expert folklorists at each stage, but they were instructed only to observe, not to hand out what Kaufman called their "competent evaluations" nor to award the usual gold, silver, and bronze medals which in the past had "warmed the participants during long winter days and evenings," a transparent plea for restoring a role that on this occasion had been stripped from folklorists. Lozanka Pejcheva, in "Folk Fest '91," describes the first "folklore holiday organized by two private firms: Uni and Total" and held atypically at an urban venue around NDK, the main cultural hall in Sofia. It featured both international and national groups, including the Kutev ensemble and a couple of village and town groups. In spite of good advertising, it attracted only a small audience, which she attributes to the as-yet-unstudied low prestige of folk music among the public. Lapsing into the rhetoric of taste and artistic quality so typical of folklorists' assessments of folklore during the communist period, she also attributes the lack of success to the "cheap" quality of the invited groups. They needed some "first-class masters" to attract an audience, an interesting put-down of the Kutev ensemble.

The 1992/2 issue, devoted to Muslim and Gypsy traditions, a once forbidden topic (especially during the hideous oppression of Muslim cultural expression from 1984 to 1989), includes "The Fire Cult among the Alevis of Northeastern Bulgaria"; "On the Folklore of the Bulgarian Muslims: Stories and Legends about Hasur"; "Birth Rituals of a Gypsy Group"; and "'Londja': a specific form of monetary cooperation among Sofia Gypsies."[4] In another obvious attempt to right past wrongs, Lora Melamed writes a profile of Milcho Leviev, Bulgaria's most renowned jazz pianist, a Jew who defected to Los Angeles and was unmentionable during the communist period.

Lozanka Pejcheva wrote two other articles during this period and in the process has emerged as a new voice among Bulgarian musical folklorists. In "An Attempt at Learning Folk Singing from the Dupnitsa Region under Nonfolkloric Conditions: An Account of One Experiment" (1992/4) she tests the efficacy of what Mantle Hood, an American ethnomusicologist, termed bi-musicality, a departure from the rather distanced observational techniques practiced by most folklorists during the communist period (though Boryana Aleksandrova had already experimented with it in the 1980s). Her three goals seem slightly naive to an American ethnomusicologist and yet represent real progress in Bulgarian folklorists' research methodology: (1) to find out if it is possible for young people born after 1950 to learn Shop singing, the most "dissonant" style of traditional Bulgarian polyphony; (2) to observe singing from the inside as another methodological perspective; and (3) to find out if the music speaks to young Bulgarians in a meaningful way. She formed a group of young people, ranging from about 20 to 40 years old, to carry out the experiment and answers her first and third questions largely in the affirmative.

In her "Observations on the Zurna Tradition in Southwestern Bulgaria" (1993/2) she studies a forbidden tradition during parts of the 1980s, in the process documenting how easily oral traditions can be undermined. One musician told her:

We here in Petrich are a little cut off from our playing. Because they told us that music with *zurnas* is Turkish. With only one sound, the police confiscated our instruments, we paid fines. That was in the period 1981–1986. After that among us it happened that we began to play in our houses. I refused to play. And many others refused. And now it is difficult yet again—because weddings are very expensive. Now urban instrumentalists (chalgadz*hii*) play—clarinets, accordions.

Another lamented, "At one time, when I heard a song, I remembered it at once. I was a god. But now I can hear it fifty times—and still I can't remember it. Now the tunes (*svirkite*) are different—not like they were in the past. Every year the style of music changes. Every year the music becomes more cultured, more contemporary."

Finally, the 1993/4 issue is devoted to the theme: "Politics and Folklore," with eleven articles on such topics as "Archaic Cultural Models and Totalitarianism," "The Road to Democracy: The Spatial Parameters of Mass Political Protest," and, rather gratuitously, Alan Dundes's "Six inches from the Presidency: The Gary Hart Jokes as Public Opinion." (But will a metric society get the joke?) Irena Bokova, in "Folklore and National Identity," argues that the association of folklore with national identity and political power has not stopped in the post-communist era, pointing to the many cultural events in towns where folklore is trotted out and introduced by local and national ministers of culture, art, and education. She reports that in the first months after November 10, 1989, folklore fell out of favor, but gradually has crept back in, and the old calendar rituals have begun to reassert themselves in the vacuum left by socialist rituals. Katya Mihailova's "Photoessay on the New Face of the Mausoleum [of Georgi Dimitrov, the first chairman of the Bulgarian Communist Party]" documents anti-communist graffiti on that monument, and Gancho Savov's "Culture as Survival among Those Sentenced for Political Crimes in the Stara Zagora Prison during the 1970s and '80s" adds to the historical record on the persecution of Muslims under the communists.

***

At the conclusion of Ankica Petrovic's paper, she seems understandably ambivalent about the future, especially given the tragedy of her native Sarajevo and Bosnia-Hercegovina. On the one hand she fears that "the collapse of the communist system" will not cause a "radical metamorphosis in the treatment of tradition in music in that part of the world." On the other hand she is hopeful that young scholars will reveal and unmask the abuses and distortions of traditional music created by political tyrants. The Bulgarian transition from communism to new forms of government has so far evolved more benignly than in the countries of the former Yugoslavia. Perhaps as a result, Bulgarian scholarship in the post-communist period from 1990 to 1993 seems to have begun a radical metamorphosis in the treatment of traditional music and folklore in at least three ways.

First, musical and folkloristic practices are now being subjected to a scholarly critique free of political manipulation. Scholars are no longer, as Petrović puts it, "constrained to ignore some connections that actually existed between and among cultures." Instead, Bulgarian folklorists are paying increasing attention to Gypsy, Turkish, and Jewish culture and the relation of Bulgarian music to Serbian and Romanian music. Second, folkloristics is no longer defined in Bulgaria as studies of rural, traditional, or "folkloric" expressions, but now includes studies of urban and popular expressive forms as well. Third, younger Bulgarian scholars are spending significant energy, as Petrović hopes, on correcting the abuses and filling in the omissions of communist-era scholarship.

From my perspective as an outsider who has traveled many times to Bulgaria over the last twenty-five years, it warms my heart to read these articles by friends and colleagues and to sense the excitement they feel at reinventing their traditions of scholarship in the service of social and cultural change rather than political stasis and control. An urgency and commitment infuses their work, which radiates a sense of personal commitment to issues of right and wrong defined in human rather than statist or communist terms. Of course, scholarship has its own forceful traditions that do not require a swing toward relevance in every instance, and Bulgarian folklorists and ethnomusicologists, surely among the most hard-working and prolific in Europe, have continued to document traditional culture in the post-communist period. On the other hand, as this review shows, there can be no doubt that from 1990 to 1993 some Bulgarian folklorists and ethnomusicologists, writing in *Bûlgarski Folklor,* charted a bold new course that will ensure the relevance of their discipline during what is bound to be a long and difficult era of national reinvention and rediscovery.

Notes

[1] Donna Buchanan, "The Bulgarian Folk Orchestra: Cultural Performance, Symbol, and the Construction of National Identity in Socialist Bulgaria," Ph.D. diss., University of Texas at Austin, 1991, contains a detailed discussion of the meanings of the word *narodna* and of the practice of *obrabotvane* ("arranging," "improving") of traditional music and dance. I am also grateful for her comments on an earlier draft of this paper. The politics of Bulgarian folklore and folk music during the communist period has also been treated in a number of other English-language sources, for example, Timothy Rice, *May It Fill Your Soul: Experiencing Bulgarian Music* (Chicago: University of Chicago Press, 1994) and Carol Silverman, "The Politics of Folklore in Bulgaria," *Anthropological Quarterly* 56(2): 55-61.

[2] The interpretations reported here are scattered in the literature and also came to me in numerous private conversations. A concentrated collection of them appears, perhaps not coincidentally, in the 1989 issue of the bulletin of the Union of Bulgarian Composers, *Muzikalni Horizonti* 12-13, as part of a collection of papers on the theme, "Professionalism in Folk-Musical and Medieval-Singing Practice."

[3] All the articles cited come from *Bulgarski Folklor*, and authors, volume numbers, and page numbers, where relevant, are given in the text.

[4] The mistreatment of Muslim minorities in the period from 1984 to 1989 is documented in Hugh Poulton, *The Balkans: Minorities and States in Conflict* (London: Minority Rights Publications, 1991).

MAGDA ZELINSKA-FERL

Response to Ankica Petrović

Ankica Petrović remarked in her paper that written records of traditional culture in Slavic lands were sporadic until the nineteenth century when, in the context of "movements for national self-recognition," traditional culture was explored in terms of strengthening national feeling. Folk culture in the nineteenth century was influenced by many factors, including the rapid change of village life due to industrialization and mass education. It is important to note that before the second half of the nineteenth century, villages in the Czech lands and Slovakia had no institutions which could systematically record folklife and its changes. This response is a breif micro-study of the development of Czech and Slovak traditional music dating from the nineteenth century to the present time, in which the "national factor" is continually at play.

In the Czech lands at the turn of this century controversy existed regarding the musical phenomena of "nationalism" and "modernism." *Česká národní hudba* (Czech national music) was understood in terms of the nineteenth century, while *česká moderní hudba* (Czech modern music) was seen as the trend of the twentieth century.[1] National music was used for the glorification of Czech and/or Slavic cultures and was viewed in terms of stability and collectivity, whereas *česká moderní hudba* was understood as a reaction of Czech music to foreign influence. While national music was seen as having the qualities of stability and collectivism, "modern music" represented discord and individualism. The composers Bedřich Smetana (1824–84) and Antonín Dvořák (1841–1904) channeled their energy and talent toward the development of Czech music, while Vítězslav Novák (1870–1949) and Josef Bohuslav Foerster (1859–1951) formed the vanguard of modern Czech music that was inspired by jazz, folksong and social poetry.

The First World War, with the decline and final dissolution of the Austro-Hungarian Empire and the creation of the first Czechoslovak Republic, contributed to feelings of nationalism in the Czech lands and Slovakia. However, as early as the 1860s there was opposition to nationalism in music. The most vocal critics were Otakar Hostinský and later Vladimír Helfert, who believed that it is the aesthetic quality in the musical work itself which is crucial to *hudební myšlení* (musical thought).[2] The 1895 Czechoslovak Ethnographic Exhibition in Prague, which for half a year displayed folklore based on three administrative regions

(Bohemia, Moravia, Silesia), was an event which resulted in "folklore fever." Some 2.5 million people visited the exhibition, including 450 Czech Americans who were presenting their folklife in a distant land.[3]

The media gave extensive coverage to the exhibition and initiated debate regarding folklore. Many believed that traditional folklore was facing inevitable extinction, and this resulted in feverish collecting and preservation. Folklore became something of a cult and its adaptation was visible in fashion, art, and architecture. This "prostitution" of folklore was criticized by such authorities as František Šalda, Joseph Machar and Miloš Jiránek, who termed it "unacceptable naturalism" and "an undesirable fad." The conviction that there is such a thing as pure and stable folklore which should not be tampered with resulted in harsh judgments such as the rejection of Janáček's opera *Její pastorkyně* (*Jenůfa*) in Prague, with the claim that this was just another attempt to be trendy.

Research into musical culture in Slovakia dates to the eighteenth century, when a monk by the name of František Vincenc Blaho (1725) made an attempt to reconstruct fifteenth- and sixteenth-century monographs. However, while Slovakia was part of the Austro-Hungarian Empire, most musical research was conducted by Hungarian scholars who were dominated by the ideology that Slovaks were an integral part of Hungarian culture.

In 1918, the Czechoslovak Republic became an independent state with Tomas Masaryk as its first president. This independence was marked by a commitment to the revival of folk traditions. Regional folk festivals, such as the Moravian Year and the Wallachian Year, enabled the people of these respective regions to investigate their cultural past. Dobroslav Orel began a systematic study into the history of Slovak music but his true research interest was Czech music. Konštantín Hudec, the first Slovak professor to devote his life to research on Slovak music, published *Vývin hudobnej kultúry na Slovensku* (The development of musical culture in Slovakia) in 1949.

In Slovakia, the nationalistic movement of the nineteenth century was led by a new generation of revivalists including P.J. Šafárik and J. Kollár. Folk music became an important element in their nationalistic orientation, and their first important publication, *Piesne swětské slowáků w Uhrách* (The secular songs of Slovaks in Hungary), was published in Pest in 1823. Four years later they published a second volume; both volumes contained a total of 220 song texts. During 1834 and 1835, *Národnié zpiewanky čili piesne swětské slowáků w Uhrách* [People's songs, or the secular songs of Slovaks in Hungary], was published with 2,500 songs. This publication is considered one of the most important folklore collections of early European Romanticism and played an important role not only with Slovak national revivalists, but also with the Czechs, Croats, Serbs, and Russians.

The generation of Ľudovít Štúr, the personage associated with the nationalist movement of Slovakia, distinguished folksong from popular tunes and encouraged the composition of social songs with nationalistic themes. For example, Samo Tomášik's text of "Hej, Slováci" later became the national anthem of Slovakia. The followers of Štúr made regular pilgrimages to Devín, a castle near Bratislava, and sang Slovak songs. The re-creation of this event heralded nationalistic tendencies which manifested themselves following the 1989 Velvet Revolution in Slovakia.

The most influential organization to contribute to the development of Slovak music culture during the 1860s was Matica Slovenska (which still exists). Its goal was, and remains, the propagation of nationalism and the strengthening of Slovak identity. The professionalization of Slovak music culture commenced after 1918, but the years 1918 through 1945 are closely tied to the development of Czech musical culture. Many institutions in Slovakia, such as *Slovenská filharmónia* (Slovak Philharmonic) and *Slovenské národné divadlo* (Slovak National Theater) in Bratislava, in reality served Czech musicians and Czech audiences.[4] For example, the first several directors of *Slovenské národné divadlo* were Czech, including Bedřich Jeřábek, who opened the theater in 1920 with Bedřich Smetana's opera, *Hubička* (The Kiss). This fact does not detract from the positive influence Czech musicians had on the development of Slovak music.

In the 1930s the most successful musical direction was *moderná*, with representatives including Eugen Suchoň, Alexander Moyzes and Ján Cikker. In contrast to Czech lands, the debate in Slovakia over "nationalistic" vs. "modern" music did not become an important issue until after 1945 when a young composer and theoretician, Ferenczy, analyzed and criticized the *moderná* movement for its ethnocentric tendencies. He encouraged the fusion of Slovak national music with the world's music, seeking inspiration from the works of Bartók, Stravinsky, and Hindemith.

The formation of the Slovak state in 1939 and the Second World War had significant influence on the development of Slovak music. One consequence was the departure of Czech musicians from Slovakia, among whom were Orel, Nedbal, and Folprecht, who contributed greatly to Slovak musical development. As nationalism reached its peak, musical life in the towns and villages turned towards dance music, which was interpreted on the basis of folklore and influenced by Gypsy musicians.

From 1945 to 1989, the development of the traditional arts and music, with research and methodology, paralleled other socialist countries, as mentioned in Ankica Petrović's paper. Numerous state-based folklore ensembles came into existence, employing traditional expressions from the past. In the re-creation of traditional dance and music the choreographers incorporated complex new arrangements, modeling them after Soviet state ensembles. These groups enjoyed considerable support from the Communist Party and the state-run media, and worked under the umbrella of large industrial plants. However, a few folklore ensembles functioned independently, their members learning various expressions of folklore orally and by example from the older generation. These ensembles would perform for local audiences at small folk festivals and various festive events.

The direction of traditional arts and music in the Czech lands and Slovakia took a very different direction after 1989, and especially after 1993, when Czechoslovakia was divided into independent and separate Czech and Slovak Republics as a result of strong nationalistic influences. Czech and Slovak intellectuals, along with the artistic community, played a decisive role in the events of the 1989 Velvet Revolution, in which artists and musicians became the catalysts of change, transformation and future direction. Václav Havel, a playwright, writer, philosopher, and a lover of folk-rock, became the president of a new democratic Czechoslovakia.

As the people of Czechoslovakia became an integral part of the global village, fear of losing their individual identity accelerated. After the divorce of the Czechs and Slovaks in 1993, nationalism manifested itself in many spheres of life, including folklore. The search for a separate identity strengthened the revival of folk traditions such as dulcimer bands, bagpipe ensembles, "tramp" songs, pub songs, and Romany popular music. Due to many factors, particularly historical events, Czech and Slovak folklore today continues to be conceptualized regionally.

As previously mentioned, the leading members of the Communist regime in 1948 turned folk music into state music in an effort to highlight the purity of socialism and thus condemn the influence of corruptive music from the West e.g., American rock-and-roll. However, only "politically correct" folk music was accepted. It was then interpreted, stylized, and choreographed by the culture specialists. Such music was disseminated over the radio and state television, in schools and various large and small public venues. However, "the everyday folk," including the youth, did not appreciate this new expression.

When the American folk singer, Pete Seeger, came to Prague in

1963 he was astounded by the number of musical groups who favored and mastered American folksongs over Czech (Černý 1995:55–57). Some believe that Seeger had a direct influence on the development of acoustic rock groups known as *folkníci* who dominated the musical scene of the 1970s and 1980s. These performers used Czech folk songs in their repertoire. Such music was less traditional and more spirited and, therefore, was preferred to the tiresome state ensemble musical palette.

Inspired by two British folk-rock groups of the early 1970s, Fairport Convention and Steeleye Span, the symbiosis of rock-and-roll and Czech folksong took place. The influence of Jethro Tull and Ian Anderson on Czech musical groups manifested itself in the development of a "harder," more electric form of folk-rock. The musicians used new instrumental combinations that included bass, electric guitar, and percussion. Groups inspired by British folk-rock were the avant garde of the mainstream of Czech folk-rock. As their music evolved, they included more and more Czech elements. The music of groups such as Mišpacha, and folk singers like Vladimír Merta and Vlastimil Třešňák, reflected the longstanding influence of the historical, tri-ethnic societal makeup of Czechs, Germans and Jews. A popular contemporary composer and pianist, Emil Viklický, linked jazz to folksongs by combining his group with traditional folk musicians. In his album, "Rain is Falling Down" (*Prší dešť*, 1994), he added Jiří Pavlica, a traditional Moravian folk musician from the Dolňácko region and Zuzana Lapčíková, a singer, to his jazz group. At present, the bands incorporating hard rock and folk style, such as the groups Fleret and Dobrohošť, enjoy tremendous popularity. Also the solo performers and duets featuring folk, pop, and rock music have captured the interest of music lovers of smaller, intimate venues, notably guitar player Dagmar Andrtová and violinist Iva Bittová who perform internationally. In an effort to express contemporary lifestyles, artists became eclectic, often combining new elements with older traditional cultural traditions. The result was stylized revivals of older traditions and, in some cases, newer expressions of them.

The prevailing post-revolution ideology of "democracy" has been translated into "everyone has to make it on their own," with the resulting dissolution not only of many folk dance groups, folk ensembles, and folk art workshops, but university and government research units as well. Immediately following the Velvet Revolution, Western cultural productions inundated Czech and Slovak society. The reaction to these performances was negative and became another factor contributing to the new interest in indigenous folklore expression. The Folklore Association of the Czech Republic now lists some 12,000 active members of folklore ensembles.

Folklore in the Czech and the Slovak republics continues to be conceptualized and presented in terms of regions and regional identity. Chodsko, the most westerly region of the Czech Republic, has a folk culture resembling that of Bavaria. Chodsko celebrates its own folklore at the festival in Domažlice. The music of this region is characterized by bagpipes, a regional folk instrument. Hundreds of bagpipers from all over the continent gather to exhibit their skills in Strakonice for a yearly bagpipe festival. Southern Bohemia is dominated by brass bands and represented by the music of Blata. The most popular folklore in Moravia is from the mountainous region of Wallachia and Moravian Slovakia. The Wallachian revival of folklore traditions is influenced by the herders who inhabit the Carpathian mountains. The focal point of folklore activities here is the city of Rožnov where, each year, half a million visitors enjoy the presentation of regional folk art in the Open-Air Museum.

One of the oldest and largest European folklore festivals is in the town of Strážnice in the region of Moravian Slovakia. Along the Slovak border lies the Horňácko region which consists of ten villages in which traditional forms of folklore flourish. Many outstanding performers, including Romany musicians, nurture traditional folklore, especially music and dance. In northern Moravia, the town of Opava represents Western Silesia, which is inhabited by Czechs, Poles and Germans. The local folklore reflects this urban, multicultural environment. Eastern Silesia is influenced by a blend of Slovak mountain and Polish border culture, with bagpipes as the musical instrument of choice.

Most regional folksongs enjoying national status originate in Moravian Slovakia, Wallachia, and Chodsko. Czech and Slovak national television is an important vehicle for the dissemination of folk culture and often feature groups from those regions. One of the most popular bands, the Moravanka Brass Band, has been imitated by many other groups throughout the Czech and the Slovak Republics.

The oldest and largest festival in Slovakia, founded in 1954, is the Východna Folklore Festival. Each year regional Slovak traditional folklore is presented to hundreds of visitors. Excluding the western region nestled against the White Carpathian Mountains, all other regions predominantly use the "cimbalovka" ensemble consisting of cimbalom, double bass, accordion, and string instruments. In these regions of Slovakia the distinctive sounds of the *fujara*—a shepherd's flute, *gajdy*—bagpipes, and various other pipes and flutes can be heard as accompanying instruments. The festival organizers traditionally invite international groups and Slovak performing groups from abroad, such as the Šarišan Slovak Dance Group from Detroit under the artistic direction of Milan Straka, the Toronto Slovak Dancers led by Milan Popík, and the Východná Dancers of Toronto with Ignac Zajac.

The most popular regional festival is the Folk Festival at Poľana, Detva, which represents folklore of the central Slovakian region. The symbol of musical expression in this region is the *fujara*, which represents mountain culture but is also considered a national folk instrument that symbolizes Slovakia itself, with over 200 *fujara*-makers in the country. Both the central and western regions are unique for their use of the rim-blown pipe, flute, and shepherd's horn. June 1995 marked the thirtieth anniversary of the Eurofolklor and the Upper Hron Festival of Song and Dance, which took place in the cities of Banská Bystrica, Brezno, and Helpa. The western region of Slovakia includes the areas of Myjava and Skalnica and presents their culture at the yearly festival in Myjava, four miles from the Moravian border, at the Myjava Folklore Celebration.

There are sizeable minorities of Hungarians, Poles, Ukrainians, Ruthenians, and Romanies in the Slovak Republic who celebrate their own cultural heritage. The northern part, alongside the West Beskydy mountains, is the home of a Polish minority whose members celebrate their traditional folklore at *Goralské folklórne slávnosti* (Goral folklore celebrations) in the town of Skalice each June. Their music is influenced by the mountain culture as personified by the sounds of various pipes, but stringed instruments are also an integral means of musical expression.

The southern part of Slovakia is occupied by the Hungarian minorities who are known for their unique sounds of cimbalom music. To acknowledge the importance of the Hungarian minorities in Slovakia, Michal Kováč and Árpád Göncz, the Slovak and Hungarian presidents respectively, attended a festival of the ethnic Hungarian minority in the southern Slovak town of Gombasek in 1994.

Ruthenians and Ukrainians, who occupy the easternmost part of Slovakia, celebrate their folklore in the cities of Svidník at *Slávnosti kultúry Rusínov* (Celebrations of the Ruthenian culture) and Ruska Poruba at *Folklorné slávnosti Rusínov* (Folklore Celebrations of the Ruthenians). PULS (Dukla's Ukrainian Folk Group) represents Ruthenian and Ukrainian folklore and, as with most Slovak folk ensembles, the *cimbalovka* (hammered dulcimer group) is the predominant means of musical expression.

Romany cultural associations organize many events to promote Romany traditions such as basket-weaving, wood-carving and blacksmithing. *Ahinsaroma* (Bratislava) is one of the societies whose members are involved in the revival of Romany culture, and they support the development and growth of many ensembles and singing groups by organizing regular practices and workshops and engaging professional Romany dancers, choreographers, and musicians at different festivals and cultural events. Other Romany organizations developing cultural activities include the Cultural Association of the Romany Community (Humenné), Roma Gemer (Rožňava) and *Romani kultúra* (Bratislava).

Presently, the people of the Czech and the Slovak Republics are undergoing a transition in every aspect of their community life. Correspondingly, the processes of folklore are being shaped at an accelerated rate and reflect the drastic social and political changes affecting every individual on both a private and public level.

On March 14, 1995, Václav Havel, president of the Czech Republic, delivered an address to the Czech Parliament. The following excerpt sheds some light on the future direction of Czechs and Slovaks in their approach to folklore:

> I would like to call attention to the fact that culture is a fundamental instrument of a self-confident society. The measure of our accomplishment in any endeavor depends on the state of our spirit, on our self-awareness, on the manner in which we are free and responsible. We cannot only proclaim individual freedom and at the same time overlook the framework in which a human being clearly understands and articulates individual freedom. We cannot rely on the background, ethics, fantasy, and self-confidence of a citizen, and at the same time overlook the circumstances from which this individual originates. Culture belongs neither to the basic foundation of society nor to its superstructure. Culture is everywhere and influences everything.

Notes

[1] Information on the *moderná* movement is from the presentations at the 1983 musicology conference in Bratislava and *Československá vlastivěda, díl IX*, 227–260.

[2] Otakar Hostinský (1847–1910) is a well-known theoretician and aestethician and the founder of the Czech musicology and aesthetics school.

[3] From Langer (1995:49). Langer is an ethnographer, historian, and the assistant director of the Wallachian Open-Air Museum. In his article he uses a geographical approach to folklife.

[4] *Československá vlastivěda, díl IX.*, 354–67.

Selected Discography

Chodská antologie. 1970. Supraphon (Czechoslovakia).
Merta, Vladimír. 1991. *Chtít chytit vítr*. VM 0003 4311.
Podpoloanie: Panorama ľudovej hudobnej kultúry. 1986. Opus
9117 1541-44.
Radhošt. 1993. *My jsme Valaši (Cimbalová muzika)*. R&S (Czech
Republic).
Slovak Instrumental Folk Music-Anthology. 1882. Opus 9117 1021.
Točkolotoč. 1989. *Chave Svitavendar*. Panton 810661 4311.

ANKICA PETROVIĆ

Response to Silverman, Rice, and Zelinska-Ferl

The responses of three scholars to my paper, "The status of Traditional Music in Eastern Europe" by Magda Zelinska-Ferl, Carol Silverman, and Timothy Rice offer different approaches to, understandings of, and interests in this topic. However, each of them, in providing a more or less direct response, offers new observations, reviews, and conclusions related to my exposition and thereby extends our focus in comprehending East European music. Their responses lend additional proof to most of my statements and open up new perspectives in the interpretation of folklore in Eastern Europe.

Magda Zelinska-Ferl, without directly commenting on my presentation, offers an historical review of the development and status of folk culture in Czech and Slovak lands. Her paper is informative on the treatment of Czech and Slovak national music, at the same time filling out our general knowledge of the status of traditional music in Eastern Europe and emphasizing the significance of Czechs and Slovaks within East European nationalist movements. A sentence in the initial paragraph of her response asserting that "before the second half of the nineteenth century, villages in the Czech and Slovak lands had no institutions which could systematically record folklife and its changes," seems not to be wholly pertinent to the discussion, since such institutions did not exist anywhere in the world.

But I found very significant Zelinska-Ferl's comments on the creation of new musical genres in Czechoslovakia that were influenced by American and British rock-and-roll music, resulting in a new symbiosis of folk-rock style in the early 1970s. In fact, such cultural phenomena became the trend among youth in most East European countries because these young people created new hybrid musical styles and genres. Depending on the country, they were more or less condemned by the official communist cultural establishment. For example, the media in the former Yugoslavia (radio-television stations and recording companies) were very benevolent towards this and other styles of new music because they produced huge commercial profits. At the same time, this music was outside the realm of "serious treatment" and scholarly recognition (Vidić-Rasmussen 1995). The consideration of such newer musical changes and an explanation of the negative political judgements relate to my previously expressed criticism of the official cultural supervision imposed by the communist systems.

I consider Zelinska-Ferl's analysis of the status of music after the "Velvet Revolution" and after the separation of Czech and Slovak lands to be most important. She explains how new social processes were reflected in culture in the form of the dissolution of artistic groups, and of "university and government research units." It is a pity that she does not supply more information on the meaning of the dissolution of the university and governmental units and how current "official" cultural politics were affected by this process. However, the final part of Zelinska-Ferl's response demonstrates how music reflects the fragmentation of a society—from "double-national" Czechoslovakia, to "single national" Czech and Slovak republics, and to further segmentation into "regional" and "marginal" cultures.

Carol Silverman's response relates most directly to my explanation of the treatment of music in the communist and post-communist period in Eastern Europe. She notes my analysis of the direct implication of that political system in the treatment of folklore and traditional music, while pointing to parallel statements excerpted from the recently published article, "The Crisis in Soviet Ethnography," by the Russian scholar Valery Tishkov. Silverman offers many other supportive facts relating to our critical judgment of previous cultural politics in Eastern Europe and presents examples of political issues in music, and of issues of music and politics, in other societies and periods. One of her crucial points is that music mobilizes all kinds of societies—for both official and subversive purposes.

I agree with Silverman's analysis. However, when I mentioned "the very innocence" of traditional music in the context of "subversive purpose," she disagreed. I have to explain that there I was expressing the opinion that not every folksong must necessarily be politicized at its origin by its character, meaning, and message, nor by its ethnic, religious, social, cultural, economic, and geographic connection. It is true, however, that the musical form or instrument identifies a particular society, culture, epoch, and region. When doing so it still may reflect "innocent" sentiments without political connotation. A further process of generating musical meaning depends on other social catalysts, whether they channel a folk song as a "strong political" or "less political" subject. It is this "less political" subject that I called "the very innocence" in traditional music. I would also repeat my assertion that each musical form may change its symbolic meaning and acquire strong political connotation under changed or exaggerated situations when it is taken over or misused by politics of a society (Petrovic 1994, 1996). I hope that a slight difference in Silverman's and my understanding of the political nature of music does not diminish our mostly shared agreement concerning the status of Eastern European traditional music and inter-reference with society.

Timothy Rice's response is addressed exclusively to interpretation of the role of the Bulgarian folklorists in the communist and post-communist periods. When giving a short explanation of their work under the communist system, he found it important to stress the differing positions of foreign and East European scholars. Rice emphasized that foreign scholars were also faced with "terror," being supervised and controlled by the local officials. However, he stressed that "we could always leave." That was one of the crucial differences between the positions of "outsiders" and "insiders" when dealing with East European culture. Outsiders could return home with their fieldwork material and elaborate on it freely, according to their theoretical orientation and other sources of information, and publish in the West.

In contrast, during the communist period, East European folklorists were officially limited in choice of theoretical orientation and of scholarly interests. All aspects of their scientific work from the "creation of idea" to finalization were supervised by the political authorities in the field.

Timothy Rice showed through several examples that the recent collapse of the communist system in Bulgaria led to the liberation from centralized cultural control of some endangered traditions (Turkish, Jewish, Gypsy) as well as the liberation of scientific thought. On the basis of the analyzed articles published from 1990 to 1993, Rice presented a new course of direction in Bulgarian folkloristics and ethnomusicology. It is marked by a freedom from political manipulation, redefinition of the discipline in the sense of the extension of scholarly interests to urban and popular studies and, to paraphrase Rice's statement, by correction of the "abusive scholarly omissions" of the previous period. Various approaches recently developed in Bulgaria are based on the different ways that scholars have related to the new political situation and also to the previous communist system.

For me, it is extremely interesting to follow the presentation of current streams of discourse by Bulgarian ethnomusicologists who were leaders in previous system—Todor Dzidzev, Todor Ivanov Zhivkov, and Nikolaj Kaufman. In their latest writings they express critical or adjusted statements about previous and future works under new political conditions (Zhivkov and Dzidzev), or the open recognition of own ethnic and cultural identity (Kaufman).

According to Rice's judgment we can conclude that the younger generation of Bulgarian ethnomusicologists and folklorists are now serving as catalysts within a changed political situation. They appear to have an understanding of all existing ethnicities, cultural practices, and processes.

Rice's statement, relating to the contemporary situation in Bulgaria, offers a more optimistic viewpoint for future perspectives than I expressed in my conclusion *vis-à-vis* the treatment of folklore in Eastern Europe. However, I also expressed a hope that the young generation of East European scholars (who have no personal connection with the political past) can forge ahead in the direction of objective interpretation of traditional and new music, as well as of relevant processes. I believe that it can happen if these young scholars can maintain their political freedom and a sense of the value of ethnic and cultural pluralism.

RONELLE ALEXANDER

Closing Comments

In November of 1989, the world began to turn upside down. Those who had lived their lives within what used to be known as the "Eastern bloc," as well as those who had dedicated their lives to studying this region, suddenly had to start all over again. The Berlin Wall came down, and in its wake began to crumble, one by one, political systems that until the day before had seemed entrenched in stone and ready to endure till the end of time.

There has been much said in the ensuing years about these radical changes, and much remains to be said. The value of the present conference is that it has focused on folklore and musicology, on aspects of the popular culture that seemed to many on the outside to have been unaffected by the rigors of politics. This of course is not true: all who understand popular culture know that it is a highly political (and often politicized) field. Folklore is an expression of the "folk," and whether they like it or not, the "folk" are the stuff of politics.

How have the "folk" and their lore become the tool of these regimes, and how have scholars of folklore coped with these facts of life? What can they say to us now that they are free to speak more openly? And what can we say to them in return? Then, both of us having spoken to each other, how do we decide where we go from here? These are the questions this conference has addressed, and it has done so in a well-formed and highly effective manner. Both in terms of geography and in terms of discipline, the scope has been extremely broad. Nevertheless, the questions have remained direct and focused. It is to the organizer's great credit to have accomplished all of this in a single day's conference.

Papers in a book often give a greater sense of balance than they did at the conference where they were read. In the case of this conference, however, the sense of balance was present from the beginning: the conference itself was like a well-composed piece of music. The morning session centered on the former USSR, and the afternoon session on the so-called Eastern Europe. Each session began with a keynote paper, in which native scholars spoke movingly about their experiences as professional folklorists and/or ethnomusicologists within a totalitarian society. Zemtsovsky and Kunanbaeva gave a chilling account of folklore under communism throughout the Soviet period, and Petrović gave a more distanced, but still sobering account of ethnomusicology in Eastern Europe.

Each paper was then followed by three responses. Here too, there was a balance: the first response was by a Western scholar who took it as her task to place the first-person accounts into a broader theoretical frame. In the morning session, Kirshenblatt-Gimblett pointed out that while the Soviet experience may have been more brutal than most, "folklore" is never innocent; and that the collecting of folklore has almost always been used with the intent to reform (and sometimes to eradicate). In the afternoon session, Silverman brought into focus the highly political nature of music, and reminded the audience that folk music could both serve the state and be an instrument of revolt against the state; she furthermore pointed out that both of these processes had been at work before and after "the Fall."

The second response to each paper was by a native scholar now living in the West. This gave a unique flavor to the proceedings: the scholars in question were not part of the process in the same way as the keynote speakers; nevertheless they were not fully objective outside observers either. Drawing upon her own life experience, each attempted to balance out the picture drawn by the keynote speaker. While not denying the harshness of academic life in the Soviet period, Gutkin pointed out that a great deal of folklore collecting did get accomplished, and that the folk did continue to create according to their own sense of tradition, adapting themselves often in very creative ways to the presence of the "state." In the afternoon session, Zelinska-Ferl supplemented Petrović's more general account with a specific history of music collecting in the Czech and Slovak lands.

The final response to each paper was by a Western ethnomusicologist who had spent considerable time in the countries in question. Each gave a moving account of cultures (and scholars) he had come to know well, and of the difference between those who then could leave, and those who could not. In the morning session, Slobin spoke of his experiences at the Soviet-sponsored 1990 International Folklore festival in Kiev, describing the pastiche of "heritages" put forth by a country which soon after ceased to exist. In the afternoon session, Rice spoke of his work with Bulgarian folk music, and especially of the transformations seen in recent years. His presentation was the final one of the conference, and he gave a decidedly upbeat note to the proceedings, by showing how the work of the younger generation of folklorists had become free of ideological overlay.

No one who has a concern for the peoples and cultures of these lands can fail to be affected by their folk art and their music. The strength of the cultural tradition that is expressed in these art forms has given aesthetic pleasure to many in the West, and spiritual sustenance to many in the East (though the more urbanized of them might not admit to this). To those who associate such art forms with the idea of "folk purity," it may be sobering to hear of the extent to which all these forms have been, and continue to be, politically manipulated. One must look at the other side of the coin, however, and remember that folk tradition is amazingly tenacious and conservative. Despite the many ills of the totalitarian world, it did sponsor and promote the recording of folk art forms on a massive scale. Now that scholars on both sides of the no-longer-existing wall are able to study these recordings more freely, they can begin better to understand both the essence of these traditional art forms, and the ways in which they have been shaped by (and responded to) the social structure that they have survived.

It is only in the case of truly brutal social change that folklore may be changed beyond recognition. It is sobering to note that the most emotional paper of the day, that by Zemtsovsky and Kunanbaeva, came from a country which although brutalized by its past has managed to survive "the Fall" without violence. By contrast, one of the most unemotionally objective papers of the day, that by Petrović, came from a land which has practically been annihilated before our eyes in the years immediately following "the Fall." The fact that Soviet folklore may have been produced at gunpoint, on the order of politicians, makes one view the idea of "pure" folklore with considerable cynicism. But the fact that the Bosnian folk countryside has been practically "cleansed" out of existence, again on the order of politicians, and that its folklore has in the process been nearly destroyed, renders one simply mute.

The final word of the conference, therefore, belongs to Ankica Petrović, who voices the hope that younger scholars will be able to rekindle and maintain a sense of political freedom, and of the value of ethnic and cultural pluralism. I can do no more in these concluding words of the volume than to call on all scholars to support this cause in any way they can.

REFERENCES

Afanas'ev, A. N. 1986. *Narod-Khudozhnik: Mif. Fol'klor. Literatura.* Moscow: Sovetskaya Rossiya.

Aksyuk, Sergey. 1962. "Composer and Song" (in Russian). Sovetskaya Muzyka 10:20-23.

_____. 1953. "On Contemporary Russian Song" (in Russian). Sovetskaya Muzyka 11:58-59.

_____. 1950. "Notes on Contemporary Folk Song" (in Russian). Sovetskaya Muzyka 11:58-59

Alexiou, Margaret. 1973. *The Ritual Lament in Greek Tradition.* Cambridge: Cambridge University Press.

Apel, Willi. 1944. "Czech Music." In *Harvard Dictionary of Music*, 198-99. Cambridge: Harvard University Press.

Baidildaev, Mardan K. 1979. *Akyn-Zhyraular Almaty.* Kazakhstan: Academy of Science.

Bartók, Béla and Albert B. Lord. 1951. *Serbo-Croatian Folk Songs.* New York: Columbia University Press.

Bartók, Béla. 1978. *Yugoslav Folk Music*, ed. Benjamin Suchoff, 4 vols. New York: State University of New York Press.

_____. 1931. *Hungarian Folk Music*, trans. M.C. Calvocoressi. London: Oxford University Press.

_____. 1920. "Die Volksmusik der Araber von Biskra und Umgebung." *Zeitschrift für Musikwissenschaft* 2: 489–522.

Bausinger, Hermann. 1990 [1961]. *Folklore in a World of Technology*, trans. Elke Dettmer. Bloomington: Indiana University Press.

Bennigsen, Alexandre and S. Enders Wimbush. 1985. *Mystics and Commissars.* Berkeley: University of California Press and London: Hurst.

Bezič, Jerko. 1985. *Glazbeno stvaralastvo narodnosti (narodnih manjina i etnickih grupa)* [Traditional Music of Ethnic Groups—Minorities]. Zagreb: Zavod za Istrazivanje Folklora.

Brailoiu, Constantin. 1984. *Problems in Ethnomusicology*, ed. and trans. A.L. Lloyd. Cambridge, London, New York: Cambridge University Press.

Brooks, Jeffrey. 1985. *When Russia Learned to Read.* Princeton: Princeton University Press.

Buchanan, Donna. 1995. "Metaphors of Power, Metaphors of Truth: The Politics of Music Professionalism in Bulgarian Folk Orchestras." *Ethnomusicology* 39: 381–416.

Černý, Jiří. 1995. "From Folklore to Hard Rock." In *The Czech Republic: Tradition and Transformation*. Washington D.C.: Smithsonian Institution, Center for Folklife Programs and Cultural Studies.

Československá vlastivěda díl IX. 1971. Praha: Horizont.

Chicherov, V. 1938. "Skazy Marfy Kriukovoi o Lenine i Staline." *Kniga i proletarskaia revoliutsia* 1:(n.p.).

Cvetko, Dragotin. 1981. *Južni slaveni u istoriji evropske muzike* [South Slavs in the history of European music]. Beograd: Nolit.

Czekanowska, Anna. 1972–73. "The Principles of Construction of Ancient Slavic Song." *Narodno stvaralaštvo, Folklor* (Beograd) XI/XII, 44/45: 96–116.

_____. 1972. *Ludowe melodie waskiego zakresu w krajach slowianskich* [Narrow-range folksongs in Slavic countries]. Warsawa: Polskie Wydawnictwo Muzyczne.

_____. 1971. *Etnografia muzyczna: Metodologia i methodyka* [Musical ethnography: methods and methodology]. Warsaw: Panstwowe Wydawnictwo Naukowe.

Dorson, Richard. 1976. *Folklore and Fakelore.* Cambridge: Harvard University Press.

Elias, Norbert. 1982 [1939]. *The History of Manners, The Civilizing Process,* vol. 1, trans. Edmund Jephcott. New York: Pantheon.

Elschek, Oskar. 1991. "Ideas, Principles, Motivations, and Results in Eastern European Folk-Music Research." In *Comparative Musicology and Anthropology of Music: Essays on the History of Ethnomusicology,* ed. Bruno Nettl and Philip V. Bohlman, pp. 91–109. Chicago: University of Chicago Press.

_____, ed. 1980. *Stratigraphische Probleme der Volksmusik in den Karpaten und auf dem Balkan.* Bratislava: Veda Verlag der Slowakischen Akademie der Wissenschaften.

Eriksen, Thomas Hylland. 1993. *Ethnicity and Nationalism. Anthropological Perspectives.* London and Boulder: Pluto Press.

Fabian, Johannes. 1990. *Power and Performance: Ethnographic Explorations through Proverbial Wisdom and Theater in Shaba, Zaire.* Madison: University of Wisconsin.

Feintuch, Burt. 1988. *The Conservation of Culture: Folklorists and the Public Sector.* Lexington: University of Kentucky Press.

Forry, Mark E. 1986. "The 'Festivalization' of Tradition in Yugoslavia." Paper presented at the Annual Meeting of the Society for Ethnomusicology. Rochester, New York.

Geertz, Clifford. 1973. *The Interpretation of Cultures.* New York: Basic Books.

Ginzburg, Semen. 1934. *Music in the Museum* (in Russian). Leningrad: Hermitage Museum.

Gusev, Victor, ed. 1948. *The South Urals Folk Song* (in Russian).Leningrad: Academy of Science.

Hall, Stuart, and Tony Jefferson, eds. 1976. *Resistance Through Rituals*. London: Hutchinson.

Herzfeld, Michael. 1982. *Ours Once More: Folklore Ideology and the Making of Modern Greece.* Austin: University of Texas Press.

Hobsbawm, Eric and Terence Ranger, eds. 1983. *The Invention of Tradition.* Cambridge: Cambridge University Press.

Hofer, Tamas. 1991. "Construction of the 'Folk Cultural Heritage' in Hungary and Rival Versions of National Identity." *Ethnologia Europaea* 21: 145-170.

Horváthová, Katarína. 1983. *Zdroj a vývoj slovenskej národnej moderny* [The source and development of Slovak national modern music]. Bratislava: Slovenský hudobný fond.

Howell, Dana Prescott. 1994. *The Development of Soviet Folkloristics*. New York: Garland Publishing.

Hufford, Mary. 1994. *Conserving Culture: A New Discourse on Heritage.* Champaign: University of Illinois Press.

Ješko, Milan. 1988. *Slovak Music*. Bratislava: The Music Information Centre of the Slovak Music Fund.

Kaufman, Nicolai. 1968. *Njakoi obsci certi mezdu narodnata pesen na Blgarite i istocnite Slavjani* [Some General Features of Bulgarian and East European Folksongs]. Sofia.

Kirshenblatt-Gimblett, Barbara. 1990. "Problems in the Early History of Jewish Folkloristics." In *Proceedings of the Tenth World Congress of Jewish Studies, Jerusalem, 1989, August 16*, ed. David Assaf, pp. 21-32. Jerusalem: World Union of Jewish Studies.

_____.1988. "Mistaken Dichotomies." *Journal of American Folklore* 101:140–155.

Kodály, Zoltán. 1960. *Folk Music of Hungary*, trans. R. Tempest and C. Jolly. London: Barrie and Rockliff.

Krader, Barbara and Bálint Sárosi. 1993. "Southern and Eastern Europe." In *Ethnomusicology: Historical and Regional Studies*, ed. Helen Myers, pp. 160–196. New York: W.W. Norton.

Kurin, Richard. 1992. "Presenting Folklife in a Soviet-American Cultural Exchange: Public Practice during Perestroika." In *Public Folklore,* eds. R. Baron and N. Spitzer, pp. 183–216. Washington and London: Smithsonian Institution Press.

Langer, Jiří. 1995. "Vernacular Architecture in the Czech Republic." In *The Czech Republic: Tradition and Transformation*. Washington D.C.: Smithsonian Institution, Center for Folklife Programs and Cultural Studies.

Lapin, Victor. 1991. "The Destruction of Folklore and Ecology of Culture" (in Russian). *Iskusstvo Leningrada* [The art of Leningrad] 7:4-7.

Lébl, Vladimír and Jitka Ludvová. 1983. "Nová doba" [New era]. In *Hudba v českých dejinách* [Music in Czech history]. Praha: Editio Supraphon.

Levashov, Valentin. 1956. *Modern Siberian Songs* (in Russian). Moscow: Muzgiz.

Lockwood, Yvonne. 1971. "Vuk Stefanovic Kǎradzic: Píoneer and Continuing Inspiration of Yugoslav Folkloristics." *Western Folklore* 30:19–32.

Lunacharsky, Anatoly. 1919. "Ilya Muromets as a Revolutionary" (in Russian). *Plamia* 44:3-8(787-792).

Lurie, Vladimir, Vladimir Bakhtin, and Boris Putilov, eds. 1994. *Folklore and Cultural Environment of the GULAG* (in Russian). St. Petersburg: Memorial.

Manuel, Peter. 1988. *Popular Musics of the Non-Western World: An Introductory Survey*. New York: Oxford University Press.

Martin, Bernice. 1979. "The Sacralization of Disorder: Symbolism in Rock Music." *Sociological Analysis* 40(2):87–124.

Matzner, Poledňák, Wasserberger a kolektív. 1990 *Encyklopedie jazzu a moderní populární hudby*. Praha: Panton.

Miller, Frank J. 1990. *Folklore for Stalin. Russian Folklore and Pseudofolklore of the Stalin Era*. New York and London: M.E. Sharpe.

Muchembled, Robert. 1985 [1978]. *Popular Culture and Elite Culture in France, 1400-1750*, trans. Lydia Cochrane. Baton Rouge: Louisiana State University Press.

Mullaney, Steven. 1983. "Strange Things, Gross Terms, Curious Customs: The Rehearsal of Cultures in the Late Renaissance." *Representations* 3 (Summer): 40-67.

Neverdinova, V.N. ed. 1989. *Zhanry slovesnogo teksta. Anekdot. Uchebnyi material po teorii literatury*. Tallinn: Tallinnskii pedagogicheskii institut.

Noll, William. 1994. Personal Comunication with the Author, March 28.

Oinas, Felix J. 1985. "Study of Folklore." In *Handbook of Russian Literature*, ed. Victor Terras, pp. 139-142. New Haven and London: Yale University Press.

_____. 1976. "The Problem of the Notion of Soviet Folklore." In *Folklore Today: Festschrift in Honor of Richard M. Dorson*, eds. Linda Degh, Henry Glassie, and Felix Oinas, pp. 379-397. Bloomington: Indiana University Press.

_____. 1975. "The Political Uses of Folklore in the Soviet Union." *Journal of the Folklore Institute* 12:157-175.

Ozouf, Mona. 1988 [1976]. *Festivals and the French Revolution*, trans. Alan Sheridan. Cambridge: Harvard University Press.

Petrović, Ankica. [in press]. "Perceptions of Ganga." *The World of Music* (Berlin).

_____. 1994. "Music as the Subject of Political Manipulation in the Lands of the Former Yugoslavia." Paper presented at the Annual Meeting of the Society for Ethnomusicology, Milwaukee, Wisconsin.

_____. 1990a. "Women in the Music Creation Process in the Dinaric Cultural Zone of Yugoslavia." In *Music, Gender, and Culture*, eds., M. Herndon, and S. Zeigler, pp. 71–84. Wilhemshaven: Florian Noetzel Verlag.

_____.1990b. "Correlation Between the Musical Content of Jewish Sephardic Songs and Traditional Muslim Lyrics Sevdalinka in Bosnia." In *Tenth World Congress of Jewish Studies, Art Folklore and Music, Division D 2, p*p. 165–171. Jerusalem: World Union of Jewish Studies.

_____. 1988. "Paradoxes of Muslim Music in Bosnia and Hercegovina." *Asian Music* 20(Fall/Winter):128–147.

Porter, James. 1993. "Europe." In *Ethnomusicology: Historical and Regional Studies*, ed. Helen Myers, pp. 215–239. New York: W.W. Norton.

Ramet, Sabrina Petra. 1994. "Rock: The Music of Revolution (and Political Conformity)." In *Rocking the State: Rock Music and Politics in Eastern Europe and Russia*, ed. S. P. Ramet, pp. 1–14. Boulder: Westview Press.

Razumovskaya, Elena. 1991. "Sixty Years of Kolkhoz Life in the Eyes of the Peasants" (in Russian). *Zven'ia* [Links].

Rihtman, Cvjetko. 1975. "O mjestu i ulozi tradicionalne narodně umjetnosti u našem savremenom društvu" [On the Place and Role of Traditional Music in Our Contemporary Society]. *Narodno stvaralastvo, Folklor* (Beograd) XIV: 53–56: 105–108.

Robin, Regine. 1990. "Stalinism and Popular Culture". In *The Culture of the Stalinist Period*, ed. Hans Günther, pp. 15-40. London: Macmillan Press.

Rowe, William and Schelling, Vivian. 1991. *Memory and Modernity: Popular Culture in Latin America*. London: Verso.

Shuman, Amy. 1993. "Dismantling Local Culture." *Western Folklore* 52: 345–364.

Silverman, Carol. 1996. "Music and Marginality: Roma (Gypsies) of Bulgaria and Macedonia." In *Retuning Culture: Musical Change in Central and Eastern Europe*, ed. Mark Slobin, pp. 231-253. Durham and London: Duke University Press.

_____. 1989. "Reconstructing Folklore: Media and Cultural Policy in Eastern Europe." *Communication* 11:141–160.

_____. 1983. "The Politics of Folklore in Bulgaria." *Anthropological Quarterly* 56(2):55–61.

Slovkoncert. 1994. *Slovakia and its Musical Culture*. Bratislava.

Sokolov, Y. M. 1966. *Russian Folklore*, trans. C.R. Smith. Hatboro: Folklore Associates.

_____. 1941. "Osnovnye linii razvitiia sovetskogo fol'klora." *Sovetskii fol'klor* 7: 39-53.

Stoin, Vasil. 1925. *Hypothese sur l'origine bulgare de la diaphonie*. Sofia: İmprimerie de la Cour.

Synek, František. 1995. Folklorní akce české republiky 1995 [Folklore events in the Czech Republic 1995]. Praha: Folklorní sdružení české republiky.

Tishkov, Valery. 1992. "The Crisis in Soviet Ethnography." *Current Anthropology* 33:371–394.

Toporkov, Andrei, ed. 1995. *Russian Erotic Folklore*. Moscow: Ladomir.

Uçi, Alfred. 1984. The Place of Art in Socialistic Artistic Culture." In *Questions of the Albanian Folklore*, pp. 5–31. Tirana: The "8 Nentori" Publishing House.

Vidič Rasmussen, Lj. 1995. "From Source to Commodity: Newly-Composed Folk Music of Yugoslavia." *Popular Music* 14/2, 241–256.

Volkov, Solomon. 1984. *Testimony: the Memoirs of Dmitri Shostakovich*, ed. Solomon Volkov, trans. Antonina W. Bouis. New York: Limited Editions.

Von Geldern, James. 1993. *Bolshevik Festivals. 1917-1920*. Berkeley and Los Angeles: University of California Press.

Winner, Thomas G. 1958. *The Oral Art and Literature of the Kazakhs of Russian Central Asia*. Durham: Duke University Press.

Žantovská, Kristina. 1995. "Culture and Art on the Road to Democracy." In *The Czech Republic: Tradition and Transformation*. Washington D.C.: Smithsonian Institution, Center for Folklife Programs and Cultural Studies.

Zemtzovzkij, Izalij I. 1987. "Etnomuzikologija—stogodišnji put" [Ethnomusicology—a one hundred year journey]. *Narodno stvaralaštvo, Folklor* XXVI (1–4): 14–28.

_____. 1972. *Slavjanskij muzykal'nyj fol'klor* [Musical folklore of the Slavs]. Moscow: Sovjetskij kompozitor.

Zhovtis, Aleksandr. 1995. *Nepridumannye anekdoty Iz sovetskogo proshlogo.* Moscow: ITs-Granat.